# Discover the Joy

*— Exactly what you need for the journey of life*

**D. Michael Toby**

Pastor, First Baptist of Woodway, TX

# Discover the Joy

*— Exactly what you need for the journey of life*

© 2009, by D. Michael Toby

Published by The Leading Edge Publishing Company
PO Box 7411
Waco, TX 76714
www.pauljmeyer.com

Printed in the United States of America

ISBN 0-978-89811-511-6

RELIGION / Christian Life / Spiritual Growth

# Table of Contents

# Acknowledgements

First and foremost, I want to thank my wife, Jackie, for being my lifelong encourager. She has consistently been the voice telling me I should write. More than that, she has been such a wonderful source of joy and companionship making it so much easier to experience the great joys of life.

Next, I gladly acknowledge the support and encouragement of my staff at First Baptist Church of Woodway, especially my assistant and friend, Karen Livingston. She has championed this effort and worked tirelessly to edit and move this project to completion.

I truly would be remiss if I did not acknowledge the role of my long time friend, Paul J. Meyer. It was at his insistence that this project moved from concept to reality. It was his generosity that made publication possible.

Last, but not least, I am grateful for a church fellowship that has provided me an amazing place of service and has shared with me the "Joy of the Journey" so fully. It is to all of you that I dedicate this book.

Your brother,

— D. Michael Toby

# Foreword

Far too often, absolute joys offered to brothers and sisters in Christ go unclaimed.

Thankfully, we can avail ourselves of reminders from others, particularly those who've spent decades in Christian service, to make such claims. In this work, Dr. D. Michael Toby, my friend for almost a quarter-century, shares with us valuable suggestions concerning our drinking more often from joy's fountain—if we but practice what he preaches.

In this book of discovery, he offers deep, yet ever so practical, insights from the teachings of the Apostle Paul. His life experiences, and those of others he has known, are framed against the backdrop of this mighty Biblical figure who was extraordinarily capable, as well as determined, to find joy in whatever circumstances he encountered.

During his ministry of some forty-two years, Dr. Toby has learned to identify and claim joys at every hand. Speaking of, he's a "good hand" in providing this "how-to" guide for us to claim a bunch of joys for our own!

His credibility has been proven, time and again. His enthusiasm and unique Christian witness are admired and genuine. And his work at First Baptist Church of Woodway is the stuff of which legends are made. Ask members of the flock there, and they'll tell you how much they appreciate their pastor of thirty-two years.

Early in our friendship, he preached all services of our campus revival, despite our urging him to return to Waco, where his mother was extremely ill. He would not. She died within a week of his last service with us. Later, he was an active, supportive and effective member of the HPU Board of Trustees.

Mike and Jackie Toby are so easy to love! And to kid, a couple of years ago, friends gathered for HPU graduation exercises, during which Mike was awarded the honorary Doctor of Divinity Degree. At a fun-poking luncheon following, the Toby's son, anesthesiologist Dr. Josh Toby of Tyler, made a wry comment: "I'm glad we now have two doctors in the family to put people to sleep!"

I was privileged to read this manuscript, and to claim from it a stronger awareness of Paul's teachings, as well as deepen my appreciation for purposeful pursuits of joy, a journey in which we can all be enthusiastic participants.

Dr. Mike Toby is a minister I could not respect more. And a friend I could not value more. His is a life of all-out, sold-out picture of Christian service. Mike does nothing halfway, except perhaps in his golf game. No matter. Show me a good avocational golfer, and I'll show you one who is seeking too much joy outside the boundaries of his call....

Dr. Don Newbury
Chancellor
Howard Payne University

# Introduction

It is my intention to give you the most amazing, rewarding gift that you will ever receive. Now let me amplify on that. In actuality, it is my prayer that I will be able to facilitate your discovering that most amazing gift: the gift of God's joy characteristically in you.

We will look at 10 different aspects of joy that come to us as a result of letting Jesus be Lord of our lives.

Joy is, in fact, a spiritual gift. It comes to you when you have allowed Jesus to have control, when you have surrendered your heart to say, "I want to do your will. And I am prepared to live my life your way."

Joy is a quality that is hard to define:

- It's an intangible that makes all of the difference in life.

- It is that quality that absolutely enriches relationships we have with one another.

- It transforms circumstances into occasions of growth and blessing.

- It causes us to be able to see victory in what otherwise might be perceived as discouragement and defeat.

- It is in getting our hands on this amazing gift of joy that we are lifted out of depression, and we are able to avoid many of the pitfalls that would otherwise befall us as we go through the difficulties and uncertainties of life.

When we define joy, it helps us discover it, and that is my hope for you.

— D. Michael Toby, Senior Pastor
First Baptist Woodway, TX

# CHAPTER 1

# The Joy
# in Friendships

These are very interesting times.

In a study done in 1984 by the University of Chicago, it was revealed that Americans, on average, had three individuals with whom they could confide, no matter how important the issue might be.

Only three!

The same study, redone in 2004, revealed that the number of trusted confidants had decreased to two people.

Now only two!

But maybe even more telling is that in 1984, 10% of those interviewed said they had no one they could call a personal friend. By the year 2004, that number had risen to almost 25%!

That means one-out-of-every-four adults in our community would say:

- I don't have anyone I could name as a close friend, as a valued person in my life.

- I don't have anyone with whom I can face the struggles of life.

- I don't have anyone to confide in when I'm going through difficulties.

- I don't have anyone with whom to celebrate when I'm going through good times.

## True friends are a rare commodity

I think it is fair to say that when we talk about friendships, if you have had a handful of deep, close, enriching friendships through your lifetime, you are blessed.

A true close friend is a rare commodity, and I understand that. I am not saying you ought to have 30 close friends in life. But at the same time, I believe that one of the dynamics of Christian fellowship, one of the hallmarks of being meaningfully involved in the family of God, is that you have a growing circle of meaningful friendships.

> I believe that one of the dynamics of Christian fellowship, one of the hallmarks of being meaningfully involved in the family of God, is that you have a growing circle of meaningful friendships.

When you are in the family of God, there is that constant opportunity to meet new people and become engaged with them in the journey of life. And you are able to contribute to them through that friendship, and they in turn are contributing to you and enriching your life and your journey along the way.

It might seem an unlikely subject in the opening verses of Philippians to deal with this matter of friendship; but, the fact is, Paul exudes a joy in writing this letter to "Dear Friends." And he, almost on a subliminal level, is helping us gain some perspective on this matter of friendship.

If you have a strong and growing circle of close friendships, let this study remind you of how truly blessed you are. Hopefully, it will also affirm the things that strengthen and enrich your friendships.

If you are the one-in-four who does not have anyone, a close connection, my prayer is that you will be asking yourself:

- Lord, what have I failed to do?

- Where am I lacking in my Christian life in making myself available for friendship?

- How can I demonstrate the kind of friendship that brings reciprocation from others towards me?

We can learn from Paul's example, as well as from what he said in Philippians 1:1-8.

> *Paul and Timothy, bond servants of Christ Jesus, to all the saints in Christ Jesus who are in Philippi, including the overseers and deacons: Grace to you and peace from God our Father and the Lord Jesus Christ* (1:1-2).

I was struck by the fact that Paul's greeting begins with a declaration of friendship: his great friendship with Timothy. The fact is that when we think of Paul, we often think of him in connection with one of his friends. There was Paul and Barnabas, Paul and Silas, Paul and Timothy, Paul and Luke, and the list goes on. Do others readily identify you with your friends?

Well, we have just gotten started. Pay close attention to this. It is from a close friend writing to friends:

> *I thank my God in all my remembrance of you, always offering prayer with joy in my every prayer for you all, in*

11

*view of your participation in the gospel from the first day until now. For I am confident of this very thing, that He who began a good work in you will perfect it until the day of Christ Jesus. For it is only right for me to feel this way about you all, because I have you in my heart, since both in my imprisonment and in the defense and confirmation of the gospel, you all are partakers of grace with me. For God is my witness, how I long for you all with the affection of Christ Jesus* (1:3-8).

Let me offer four truths about friendship.

## #1 — Friends are people you remember

Paul wrote, "I thank my God in all my remembrance of you."

Remembrance is a *passive* way in which we reflect on our friend-

> Friends are people you remember.

ships as we think about those who are important to us. Hopefully, when you think about them, there is a satisfying "warm feeling" remembering how folks are precious to you and how you are precious to them is an edifying experience.

For some of us, it may be helpful to develop a selective memory. Ask the Lord to help you remember the many positive moments and to grant you the grace to let go of the disappointments.

It's human nature to remember all the hurts, all the disappointments, all the things they didn't do that you thought they should have done or could have done for you, right?

And if you are not careful, you will lose the joy of those friendships.

My hope is that you will learn how to reflect on and to think of friendships in a positive way. Dwell on those aspects of your friendship that are really rewarding, and you will find that you are able to build on past joys spent together.

In addition to the passive side of thinking about your friends, there is also an *active* side. Do you know what is going on in their lives? Have you thought about communicating in some way how much you care for them?

On a very practical level, you could demonstrate your friendship by:

- offering to baby sit so your friend can get a break

- taking a meal to them when they are sick

- sending them a note of encouragement or a note of celebration over something good that has happened in their lives saying, "Hey, we have gone too long without spending time together. Why don't you guys come over to the house, and let's have dinner?"

Don't take your friends for granted. Make a point to celebrate with them and let them know they are indeed important people in your life.

My mom had a great sense of humor, and she was a true friend to so many in our community, particularly in our church in Pasadena, Texas. A close friend of hers, Maxine Blair, was one of the secretaries at the church. Maxine had this ritual of going home every day for lunch so she could watch her favorite soap opera. She was absolutely addicted to her soap opera, and she wouldn't miss it for the world!

One day on a particular episode of the soap opera, a key character was killed. My mom sent Maxine a sympathy card, expressing her condolences that the character had passed away. Maxine never forgot that humorous act of friendship. My mom knew what was important to her friend and was able to celebrate that with her.

## #2 — Friends are people for whom you pray

Let me say that another way: friends are the people who are important enough that you are willing to spend time before God on their behalf.

We use the phrase "being an intercessor" when we talk about praying for someone. I like the phrase "being an advocate" even more because you are there fighting for and waging a spiritual battle on behalf of someone else.

Prayers can be generic, like asking for God's blessing on people, for God's best in their lives, etc; but, other times you may know certain friends are facing very real difficulties. You may be seeing the spiritual battle they are facing, and you are there in the quietness of your own home asking God to equip them, asking God to help them, asking God to deliver them so they might be victorious.

> Friends are people you pray for.

That type of prayer is intense and focused, and you are the intercessor or advocate on their behalf.

I think it is important for us to realize that our relationships are nurtured when we are praying for one another and when we put friendships in the context of spiritual living. It transforms those relationships. They move to a higher level than they would have ever reached were it not for the fact that you are praying for them.

It also creates the environment where we are able to better deal with disappointments, hurts, misunderstandings, and unmet expectations that inevitably come.

Friendships are fragile. You know Satan would love to poison those friendships, and make us want to go it on our own. He would love for us to buy into that bitter spirit and write them off ... cut them out.

But that is not the spirit of Christ! That is the spirit of the world, and every time we allow that to happen, there is a damage and a collective hurt that comes to the body of Christ.

That is why we must be people of prayer. And when we do get hurt, we go to the Lord first and deal with it there with Him. We must ask for God's grace to make it possible for us to have a tender heart, to have kindness, to offer forgiveness, even as we want to receive forgiveness. It's so important for us to ask God to give us understanding and patience, even as we want to be the benefactor of understanding and patience.

It is in prayer that God makes it possible for us to give our friends the benefit of the doubt rather than simply shutting them out because of what we perceive to be bad intentions or wrong motives. The truth is, we don't really know what is in their hearts, and we don't know what the circumstances were that may have caused them to disappoint us.

When Paul said in Philippians, *"I am confident of this very thing, that He who began a good work in you will perfect it until the day of Christ"* (1:6), he was writing encouraging words intentionally. He knew the importance of friendship. He knew that friendship stimulates us to keep on growing, to be the best, and to keep on cultivating that relationship with each other and with the Lord.

The letter itself that Paul wrote was an act of encouragement. All through the letter it talks about joy and rejoicing. It just sings the very message of the victory we can have in our walk with God.

15

But where was Paul when he wrote this letter? What were the circumstances of his life when he was writing to friends and encouraging them?

He was in prison! He was facing difficult days, having completely lost his personal freedom.

It would have been so easy for him to have been self-centered and focused on his own situation; but, Paul writes to the believers in Philippi, and it is as if he says to them, "Guys, I am convinced that you are the real deal. I have no doubt that what I saw in you in that brief time we were together really was the work of God. And God did something that was so profound in you that I know you are never going to move away from it. God has some amazing things in store for you."

If someone with the stature of Paul were to say those things to you, wouldn't that be powerful medicine?

Over the years I have been with some people of influence in my life, and I can still remember some of the phrases that just took my breath away as they spoke to me with encouragement.

> When is the last time you gave someone an absolute, unqualified compliment?

One man said, "Mike, do you know what I admire about you?" Then he went on to tell me several things he admired. I was awestruck! Here was a man whom I admired so much, he was bigger than life to me, and he was speaking words of encouragement to my soul.

You can do the same thing to those in your life.

**When was the last time you ...** gave someone an absolute, unqualified compliment?

16

**When was the last time you ...** spoke to someone and said, "I want you to know how much I love you"?

**When was the last time you ...** said, "I want you to know how much I cherish being your friend"?

**When was the last time you ...** said, "I want you to know this is what you do on a regular basis that just blesses me and touches me and inspires me"?

**When was the last time you ...** wrote a note to somebody and just said, "Thank you for what you mean to my life"?

We love to receive compliments. We appreciate every word of encouragement we can get. But isn't it amazing how most of us are misers when it comes to giving others encouragement? We know how good it feels to receive it, but we are slow to reciprocate.

Why is that? We all agree it shouldn't be that way, but it is. I believe we should change that.

Paul went on to say, *"I'm sending someone whom I know is a friend of yours, Epaphroditus, he's been with me, he's been such a benefit to me, but I have the sense that you need him as your friend today more than I need him. I'm sending him to you"* (2:25, paraphrased).

This is an act of unselfishness and encouragement that Paul offers.

### #3 — Friends are people with whom you share life's greatest experiences

Listen to the language that Paul uses when he writes, *"It is only right for me to feel this way about you all, because I have you in my heart, since both in my imprisonment and in the defense and confirmation of the gospel, you all are partakers of grace with me"* (1:7).

The word "partakers" is so rich throughout the New Testament. It speaks of shared experiences and true fellowship.

I think the word "fellowship" has really lost the power of its meaning over the years. It means partnership, that something wonderful occurred to bind us together, and that we believe there is oneness that exists in our relationship.

> Friends are people with whom you share life's greatest experiences.

Paul said, "We have that kind of connection because of the partnership we have shared." "You have been with me even in my imprisonment," he said. "You are there. I know I can count on you."

I think it's sad that many adults have to go all the way back to high school, junior high, or even little league to remember what it was like to feel that kind of bond, that kind of partnership, that kind of connection with other people.

But I'm here to tell you that in following Jesus, He offers to us an amazing opportunity to partner together!

In church you study the Bible, worship, pray, learn, grow, expand, and go through life's journey together. You hear God speak and work that out, possibly with the help or encouragement of the church staff, Bible teachers, and group members. You may even go on mission trips together, further cementing your relationship together.

As a result, you form a kind of partnership. I know we have that in our church! You have those moments that open up your relationship on a level you would never have known otherwise.

I'm an absolute advocate of our home-group ministry. In a relaxed environment of homes on Sunday evening or whenever you meet, you have the opportunity to get to know one another over a meal, you have the casual give and take, and then you take time to share prayer requests and time to make application out of the Word of God. Something happens in those settings that we seldom make time for in the usual rat race of life.

If you find yourself alienated or alone, there are opportunities to connect, to forge partnerships that will last a lifetime. I challenge you to make yourself available for them.

## #4 — Friends are people you love

The Apostle Paul uses language here that is not really what you would expect from a hard-driving missionary theologian. Listen to the way he describes his feelings for the people he writes to. He says, *"For God is my witness, how I long for you all with the affection of Christ Jesus"* (1:8).

Do you think Paul said that lightly? I don't think so. Paul is saying, "You can take this to the bank! I am telling you the gospel truth."

In our self-centered world, that is not normal. We put all of our effort and prayers into what is mine, what concerns me, my interests, etc. Paul is saying that though he is a long distance away and in a prison cell, the love he has for his people has no boundaries. There is no limit to how much he can love them.

God has made it possible for you and for me to love each other with that kind of love.

> In following Jesus, He offers us that ongoing, amazing opportunity to partner together.

C.S. Lewis so accurately said, "To love at all is to be vulnerable." Would you agree with that? Love anything and your heart will be wrung and possibly broken.

19

If you want to make sure of keeping it intact, you must give your heart to no one, not even to a faithful pet. You must wrap it carefully around hobbies and little luxuries, avoid all entanglements, and lock it up safe in the casket or coffin of your selfishness.

But in that casket — safe, dark, emotionless, airless — it will change. It will not be broken, but it will become unbreakable, impenetrable, and irredeemable. What a terrible thing!"

> **Friends are people you love.**

The only place outside of heaven where you can be perfectly safe from all dangers is in hell. So many of us, either out of choice, cynicism, bitterness or neglect, have relegated ourselves to a living hell. We have cut ourselves off from the amazing joy of friendship.

Please, don't let that describe you. Find the joy of friendships!

## Take action

Now is always the time to take action.

 What can you do today to send a clear signal of appreciation and thanks to those people who are your friends?

 What do you need to do to change your schedule so you are available to reach out to others?

 What new commitments do you need to make that will remove any sense of being alone or alienated?

 What can you do today to rediscover the joy of friendships?

# CHAPTER 2

# The Joy of
# Spiritual Vitality

Unwittingly, many of us are more like artificial silk plants than we are real living plants.

How does this happen? It happens slowly in a church culture where we learn to say the right words, learn to do the right things, and learn to look like a living, breathing, joyful Christian. We try to look like we have our act together, and when we have successfully convinced others, we start to work convincing ourselves.

Or perhaps you are best described as a beautiful flower that has been cut and placed in a vase.

Somehow, somewhere, you were cut off from the very life and nourishment that produced your growth. There was a time when you were vibrant and full of life. The Lord was so real in your life that there was spiritual fruit being produced joyously and on a regular basis. But something happened, a choice was made, and now you can't stop the drying, fading process.

## You are not alone

These sad descriptions hit us all right between the eyes. Whether it's being artificial, or feeling as though our joy is fading, we have all experienced such moments. The good news is that we do NOT need to remain there!

John 15:5 says, "*I am the vine, you are the branches. He who abides in Me and I in him, he bears much fruit, for apart from Me you can do nothing.*"

> You can't help but bear fruit when you are a branch ... on His tree!

When you abide in Him, He abides in you! And as a result, you bear fruit!

There will be vitality. You will continue to draw from the very source of life and carry on growing. It will be a perpetual blessing, not only to you, but also to the world around you.

## How to maintain your spiritual growth

I believe there are five powerful ways we are able to maintain the spiritual vitality that blesses us, that accomplishes God's purposes, and that result in our having a wonderfully characteristic attitude of joy in all we do.

## #1 — Pray purposefully

There was a sign on a church door in New York that was unsettlingly shocking. It read, "Gone out of business. Didn't know what our business was."

Can you believe that?

And yet, that congregation may have been more honest than most of the churches across the land. We go through the motions, but we forget what the motions are all about and what it is we are really trying to accomplish.

The disciples grew up in the Jewish tradition and had been trained in religious ways their entire lives, but there came a point when they approached Jesus and said, "Lord, teach us to pray."

Surely they should have known how to pray with all their religious training. It would have been very easy for Jesus to say, "Oh my goodness, who is this group that I've called to follow me. You guys don't even know the most basic things about spiritual life. Do I have to start all over with you and teach you how to pray?"

But it wasn't the act of praying that the disciples needed help with, and Jesus understood that. They knew the ritual, they knew the mechanics of prayer, and they knew the philosophy behind prayer.

> Do you go through the motions and forget what the motions are all about?

What they lacked was the power they had witnessed in Jesus. They had witnessed purposefulness in the life of Jesus. Wisely, they made the connection between what they saw in Him, what they heard in Him, and what was being produced through Him, with the time He spent in prayer with the Father.

They were saying, "We want some of that too. We want purpose. We want access to that power and life. Show us how to do that."

Paul said, *"**And this I pray** ... "* (Philippians 1:9, emphasis mine).

This is not a generic prayer or a Hail Mary cover-everything type of prayer. He was intentionally praying on behalf of those he was writing to, sharing with them before the Father the things he knew would be essential to their spiritual life.

*Father, forgive me for falling into this*

## #2 — Choose to grow

Prayer is your access to spiritual vitality. Prayer is an act of your will that declares your desire for closeness and intimacy with God, where God's life is reproduced through you. It declares your desire to grow.

> Prayer declares your desire to grow.

Prayer is the vehicle, if you will, that transports us to the spiritual gymnasium where the workout of spiritual vitality begins.

When Paul said, *"And this I pray, that your love may abound,"* he followed it with, ***"still more and more ..."*** (Philippians 1:9, emphasis mine).

More and more! It's all about growth.

Jesus summarized everything that God expects of us as His children into two simple statements when He said:

> #1) Love the Lord thy God with all your heart, with all your mind, and with all your strength.

> #2) Love your neighbor as yourself.

Likewise, Paul touches on the most central aspect of what God wants for us. He wants us to have more and more love for God and more and more love for others.

Back to the gymnasium metaphor: we have all learned that in order to have a strong heart we must exercise it. This requires constant work, constant strengthening, and constant care. The benefit from this is for the rest of your life.

In order to have more love, we must exercise our hearts to love more and more. As a result:

- You will learn how to stretch and strengthen your heart so you can find your capacity to love God!

its a decision to exercise!

24

- Your spiritual life will not die, fade, or diminish as the years go by; but, instead it will grow, increase, and abound!

- God will become more real, more intimate, and more precious to you.

- What you have today is to remain fresh and vibrant.

Through prayer we can accomplish this.

## #3 — Pray so your love may abound

Paul's prayer was that our *"love may **abound**"* (1:9, emphasis mine). The word "abound" is a powerful word. He is saying that our love should be without limits, filled with energy.

I believe Paul is saying:

> Not only do I want you to learn how to love God more, but in the process you will discover that you will be loving one another with a less selfish, more patient, more consuming love than you have ever known in your life!

That is what abounding love will bring.

Jesus said that the mark of His followers would be the love that we have for each other.

When we love other people, we share what we have found to be the most important, most precious, and most true in our own life, and that is the richness of our walk with God.

> Ask God to plant you where He wants to plant you.

Paul goes on in his prayer, *"And this I pray, that your love may abound still more and more in real knowledge and all discernment, **so that you*** *might approve the things that are excellent"* (Philippians 1:9-10, emphasis mine).

Do you hear what Paul is saying:

> I hope your love abounds so you have a passion for getting into the Word of God, so you have that genuine desire to say, "Lord, teach me everything I need to know so I might live that kind of life where I make good decisions, where I'm able to make the hard decisions, even though it might not be immediately gratifying. I know long term I'm doing the right things that build a solid foundation, that put me in a place where You want me to bear fruit that brings honor and glory to Your name."

That's what spiritual vitality is all about. Knowing your life counts, knowing you are really where God wants you to be.

## #4 — Be filled with the fruit of righteousness

What is the result of being joined to Jesus and being a part of His body? The answer is fruit! You will be filled with the fruit of righteousness.

For a lot of people, their life is characterized by the following:

- Anxiety

- Materialism

- Fatigue

- Selfishness

- Lack of time with family

- Pride

- Stress

Paul tells us it is possible for us to have the kind of spiritual life where we are connected to the vine — we are drawing from the very life of Christ, like living water that nourishes and refreshes and blesses us and brings wonderfully satisfying results to us.

In short, life without regret!

What is a mid-life crisis all about? I think you can summarize that pretty easily. A mid-life crisis invariably has to do with regrets. You've lived your life up to that point and now you look at it and realize you've missed it. You've put all your energy, all your efforts, and all your resources into things that just do not satisfy.

> Live your life without regrets.

Sadly, those going through a mid-life crisis, mid-life examination, often find the worst kinds of ways to try to make their lives exciting or meaningful.

But when we have the discernment and knowledge that God wants us to have, which comes from of His word and from our abiding in Him, it makes it possible for us to live a life without regrets.

## #5 — Be sincere and blameless

Paul said that his prayer for us was that we *"might approve the things that are excellent **in order to be sincere and blameless until the day of Christ"*** (Philippians 1:10, emphasis mine).

The day of Christ refers to when Jesus is coming again, that climactic moment in all of history when all of God's children are going to be gathered home. Paul prayed that the quality of our spiritual life would result in our being sincere and blameless before the Lord.

The word "sincere" means to pass the test while under the scrutiny of direct sunlight. You see, many of us really don't want the Lord, or anybody else, to look too closely into our lives. We may not want people to check our TV cable bill to find out what we've been watching. We may not want anyone to look at our checkbook or our credit card statements to see what we've been buying.

But that lacks sincerity.

Paul prayed that we would have the kind of connectedness with the living Lord that would cause us to say, "Lord, shine your light on me." That is confidence! And when you have spiritual vitality, you have confidence.

I think deep satisfaction is one of the fruits of spiritual vitality. You have the sense that life is worth living and that you are making investments that are worthwhile. You are touching people's lives in a positive way.

There are times that I feel tired. I tell myself, "Toby, you're not as young as you used to be," but even when I say that, I can honestly say that I have never had more satisfying days than I'm having right now!

> I'd rather be tired and satisfied than energized and empty.

I absolutely love the opportunities I have to visit with so many in my congregation, to sit over a lunch table and hear how the Lord has drawn them to this place and what Christ is doing in their lives, and to share so many other experiences within the church body and local community. I know God's hand is on us.

Without question, I would rather be tired and satisfied than energized and empty. I draw on the treasured promise that *"those who wait on the Lord will renew their strength, they will mount up like eagles, they will run and not grow weary, they will walk and not faint"* (Isaiah 40:31).

That is a promise from God that I know I can claim because I'm trying my best to stay in touch, to stay vitally connected to Jesus, and I want what is happening in my life to be the result of who He is in me.

## Your lasting legacy

One of the satisfying results of spiritual vitality is a lasting legacy. What are people going to say about you when you are gone? And you know they are going to talk about you when you're gone! What are they going to say about you?

I've heard it said about a guy who died, "He was old before his time." What did they mean by that? Somewhere along the way he quit trying, he quit growing. He lost the energy and passion for life.

> Is it possible that you've become satisfied with the plastic and artificial rather than the living and growing?

Don't let that happen to you!

Then I think about others I know who are still dreaming the dreams, still setting the goals, still recognizing there is something worth living for as long as they draw breath.

What is the difference? They are still connected to the vine. They are still drawing from that life in Christ.

Remember the flowers?

Is it possible that you've become satisfied with plastic and artificial rather than living and growing? Is it possible even though well intentioned, you made the mistake of thinking that imitation was enough?

> Let God nurture you, feed you, plant you, restore you, and bring forth fruit that will amaze you!

If so, recognize that God wants to be the source of your spiritual life. You are His child. Open up and ask Him to breathe life into you, replacing the fake with the real ... and He will do it!

Or maybe you are a cut flower? Have you somehow gotten severed from the vine?

If so, it is possible for you to reconnect. Go to God and say, "Lord, You have been real to me in the days gone by. Now, Lord, forgive me for letting myself get cut off from You. I want to reconnect. I want to once again draw near. I want my life to abide in a relationship with You." And He will do it!

Let Him nurture you, feed you, prune you, restore you, and you will bring forth fruit that will amaze you!

He is, after all, the ultimate gardener.

## Take action

Now is always the time to take action.

- Pray purposefully

- Choose to grow

- Pray so that love may abound

- Be filled with the fruit of righteousness

- Be sincere and blameless

Forgive me sweet lord for choosing to try / falsely "solve" problems on my own & ∴ look & become dead. Breathe your life into me, Lord — into Sam, into Jack. Make our #1 cause to be alive for **YOU**. You Lord, are all that matters.
    In your precious name, Jesus, I pray Amen.

# CHAPTER 3

# The Joy in Difficulty

It is easy to think about the joy of friendship and the joy that comes from a vital relationship with God; but, can we find joy in difficulty?

That's not nearly as easy to see at first glance, but dig a little deeper and there truly is joy in difficulty.

## Some get it, some don't

Why is it that two people can go through very similarly difficult circumstances, yet one manages to exhibit a dignity, a strength, a positive spirit, and even the ability to say, "I have found good and made lemonade with the lemons. I have found blessing and can see how this will help me. I have purpose in the trial, and I will benefit"?

> When you are facing adversity, joy is available.

While at the same time, the other person disintegrates into a tortured soul filled with self-pity, defeat, and frustration.

When you are going through the fire, joy is available to you as a follower of Jesus. When you are facing adversity, joy is available. And when things are not easy and are not going your way, joy is available.

Some people find this joy when they are going through the storm and some people don't; but, it is available to us all.

## Preaching joy from prison

Paul wrote an amazing treatise on how to discover joy in daily living as he sat in a Roman prison. I don't think he set out to teach the five secrets of joy in difficulty, but out of his own testimony I believe there are five extremely relevant truths that will help each of us as we go through the fire.

Here is what Paul wrote:

> *Now I want you to know, brethren, that my circumstances have turned out of the greater progress of the gospel, so that my imprisonment in the cause of Christ has become well know throughout the whole praetorian guard and to everyone else ...* (1:12-13)

He is looking at the circumstances through God's eyes!

> *...and that most of the brethren, trusting in the Lord because of my imprisonment, have far more courage to speak the word of God without fear* (1:14).
>
> *Some, to be sure, are preaching Christ even from envy and strife, but some also from good will; the latter do it out of love, knowing that I am appointed for the defense of the gospel; the former proclaim Christ out of selfish ambition, rather than from pure motives, thinking to cause me distress in my imprisonment. What then? Only that in every way, whether in pretense or in truth, Christ is proclaimed; and in this I rejoice* (1:15-18).

*[handwritten annotations: "no matter the persous' motives", "overarching will", "result will be", "the Gospel-truth of who Jesus really is, will spread"]*

Based on what they believe and know, the people chose to act rather than react!

> *Yes, and I will rejoice. For I know that this will turn out for my deliverance through your prayers and the provision of the*

*Spirit of Jesus Christ, according to my earnest expectation and hope, that I will not be put to shame in anything, but that with all boldness, Christ will even now, as always, be exalted in my body, whether by life or by death (1:18b-20).*

Paul is fully secure in God, knowing that through him, God is going to accomplish His will.

*For to me, to live is Christ, and to die is gain.* (Philippians 1:12-21)

Lastly, Paul is so full of grace that it overflows out of him!

## #1 — Look at your circumstances through God's eyes

If you want to experience joy in your life in the difficult times as well as the good times, it is imperative for you to do what Paul has done, and that is to learn how to look at life and to look at circumstances through God's eyes.

It's all about perspective, God's perspective.

In order to look at your life and to look at circumstances through His eyes, you must first get to know God intimately and maintain fellowship regularly with Him. Only then will you know His heart and His love, which enables you to see and to trust what He is doing.

> It is imperative that you look at your life and your circumstances through God's eyes.

Or to put it another way, seeing through God's eyes is all about faith. It means that you are learning to recognize who God is and how God wants to relate to you in every circumstance of life.

When you place your faith and trust in God, you become convinced that:

- He is with me all the time!

- He dwells in me!

- He will never forsake me!

- He will never leave me to face the difficulties on my own!

- He will protect me!

- He will sustain me, no matter how difficult the struggle, no matter how hot the flame!

- He will comfort me through it all!

It is from this vantage point that we begin to see more clearly what is happening in our lives. As a result, an absolute, rock-solid conviction grows in us that God's desire is to ultimately bless us, to enrich us spiritually, and to use us for His glory.

Wow!

Coming to this point of faith begins with the very simple and yet sometimes difficult decision of taking your eyes off yourself and circumstances … and truly looking to God.

## #2 — Surrender yourself to God's purpose

Only when we are surrendered to God's will are we in a position to see our circumstances through God's eyes. And only then are we able to interpret our circumstances in such a way that God will guide us through for His glory.

I think it is important at this point to discuss the differences between JOY and HAPPINESS.

Happiness is something you look for, as in the "pursuit of happiness." This may be a popular phrase, but the pursuit of happiness really speaks of a self-centered life where everything is judged on how it benefits, rewards, or blesses me.

> Surrender yourself to God's purpose.

Joy, on the other hand, is something that happens to you. It is the spiritual sense of well being that comes to us as a result of knowing that we are in the will of God, that our life has the hand of God on it, and that we really are accomplishing the purpose God has given us on this earth.

Clearly stated, there is a vast difference between joy and happiness.

In *You Gotta Keep Dancing*, author Tim Hansel says, "Joy defies circumstances and occurs in spite of difficult situations." He adds, "Happiness is a feeling, but joy is an attitude. Joy is that deep settled confidence that God is in control of every area of my life."

> "Happiness is a feeling, but joy is an attitude."
> — Tim Hansel

I've often wondered if other believers ridiculed Paul as he sat in prison. After all, he was in a prison years earlier and was set free. And what about the other disciples being miraculously transported out of jail, leaving locked doors and unknowing guards behind! It was certainly within God's power to release Paul.

But no angels came to set him free, no earthquake broke the walls down, nothing. He simply sits in jail while claiming that God is a God of power!

I would be surprised if people were not mocking him, but what did Paul do?

- He continued doing what he was doing.

- He continued to trust and praise God.

- He refused to be distracted by what others said about him.

- He chose not to react to the things that were out of his control.

- He refused to get caught up in semantics and petty arguments.

- He continued to keep his eyes on Jesus.

- He continued to rejoice that the name of Jesus was being presented to a lost world.

He surrendered himself to God's purposes and stayed focused on those things. But if we are not careful, Satan will rob us of the joy that God wants us to experience because he is masterful at blinding us to the opportunities that are right in front of us.

Instead, we are to maintain focus by regularly praising God for who He is, how faithful He is, and how loving He is. We can also speak a word that builds others up, that blesses, that absolutely shouts the victory we know we have because of the faithfulness of God to meet our need.

> **You are either a victim or a gallant fighter!**

There is always the temptation for us to worry about tomorrow and to forget the blessing and the provision of today. The best medicine to combat that temptation is to immediately thank God and bless His name.

## #3 — Act rather than react

Paul chose to act instead of react to his situation, circumstances, and opportunities. We must do the same.

Tim Hansel goes on to say there are only two ways to view life: as a victim or as a gallant fighter. You must decide if you want to act or react.

Paul isn't trying to change the whole form of Roman government. Paul is saying:

> Here I am as a prisoner. I would have never dreamed it, would never have envisioned it in my own limited wisdom, but I'm finding God is able to use me in this setting in a way that I never could have been used otherwise.

THAT is the heart and mind of a gallant fighter, not a victim.

Are you going through the fire right now? Are you in the middle of great difficulty? If so, then I encourage you to pray:

- God, what is it You want me to do in this situation?

- Lord, is there someone You want me to reach out to help right now?

- God, is there someone You want me to speak to?

- Lord, how can I bless somebody else as I go through my day?

Whining and complaining have a way of sneaking in on us as the fire heats up; but, like Paul, we need to choose how we will respond: act the victor or react the victim. When Paul tells us to rejoice, he is challenging us to reject self-pity and choose the better way.

As a result of his imprisonment, Paul points out, *"... the cause of Christ has become well known throughout the whole praetorian guard ..."* (1:13).

Here were the Roman soldiers in the governor's palace, the most feared perhaps in all of Rome, now coming under the power of Christ!

Paul adds, *"... most of the brethren, trusting in the Lord because of my imprisonment, have far more courage to speak the word of God without fear"* (1:14).

Good, great good, was coming as a result of his imprisonment. And Paul boldly embraces it!

How could Paul do this? Because he had fully given his life over to Christ. I believe that is one of the main reasons why most people never see the good in their fire, crisis, and difficulty ... because their lives are not fully devoted to God!

Romans 8:28 is a verse that many of us hold on to. It says, *"And we know that God causes all things to work together for good ...."*

That is where most of us want to stop. We want to believe that we have God's promise to bless us and always bring us good. But that is only part of the verse, and it is a conditional promise.

Here is the full verse: *"And we know that God causes all things to work together for good to those who love God and to those who are the called according to His purpose"* (8:28).

That changes things!

So, if you really want to act rather than react, if you want to know joy on a day-by-day basis, if you want to discover joy when you are going through the difficult times of life, then you must be sure your love for God is intact and that you really are surrendered to His purposes for your life.

## #4 — Be secure in Him

Another way that Paul maintained his joy in the middle of his difficulty was this: Paul was secure in God.

Sure, Paul's future was very much in doubt. In fact, Paul was ultimately martyred, but day to day in that jail cell, Paul knew he was securely in the palm of God's hand.

He wrote: *"I know that this will turn out for my deliverance through your prayers and the provision of the Spirit of Jesus Christ, according to my earnest expectation and hope, that I shall not be put to shame in anything, but that with all boldness, Christ will even now, as always, be exalted in my body, whether by life or by death"* (1:19-20).

I see a paradox here, and no doubt you do as well.

Paul explains how many believers have made bold decisions because of his confinement, and how many people (i.e. the Roman guards) who would not normally hear the message of Jesus are

> **You can be secure and know whose you are and where you are, but not know where you are going!**

in fact forced to hear Paul speak, and in both cases the results have been great. He is a prisoner, but lives are being affected for the glory of God.

Then, in the next breath, Paul writes that he longs for, expects, and asks people to pray for God to set him free.

Clearly, joy in difficulty does not mean that you do not want things to change, that you do not want your circumstances to improve, or that you deny the difficulty of your situation.

Rather, you want your circumstances to change, but you place that desire second to the will and purpose of God.

What's more, it's not a matter of being Pollyanna, of having a smile on your face and acting as though you're not facing terrible, adverse moments in your life. It's not a matter of choosing to be ignorant of the facts.

No, it is having a smile on your face in spite of your very real circumstances. That is the "nevertheless" that is full of faith, trust, and hope.

Paul is a great example of how to be real in the midst of trouble, and how to remain secure in our God who loves us every second of every day.

## #5 — Walk in the grace that God provides

All of us can recall times in our lives that seemed as though they would never end and yet, when we look back, as painful as they were, they are now just a dim memory. Perhaps we have chosen to push them out of our memory bank. The truth is that they were so stressful, so hard that we weren't sure we would survive. And yet God brought us through.

That is the grace of God, and in the middle of great difficulty, you can rest assured that God's grace is there for you.

My hope is that we would, as James wrote, be able to *"count it all joy when you encounter various trials, knowing those trials produce endurance"* (James 1:2-3).

42

How can you possibly "count it all joy?" It is only possible when you walk in the grace that is yours.

> **God's grace is right there in the midst of your battle**

The reality is, in the midst of your difficulty, you are uniquely positioned to see God work and to allow God to use you for His honor and glory?

Paul took all of this into account when he, full of grace, prayed, "… *according to my earnest expectation and hope, that I shall not be put to shame in anything, but that with all boldness, Christ shall even now, as always, be exalted in my body, whether by life or by death. For to me, to live is Christ, and to die is gain"* (1:20-21).

In the midst of hardship, Paul wants to do what God has for him. Grace!

In the midst of his chains, Paul does not want to bring embarrassment to the name of Jesus. Grace!

In the midst of a bleak future, Paul asks his supporters to pray for him that he may further the cause of Christ and bring glory to His name. Grace!

How many of us, in our most unfair, unjust, and unimaginable times are saying, "God, give me grace to be able to reveal Christ to those who are watching me as I go through this"?

We can, through God's grace.

## Choose joy

Clearly, joy is a choice! Paul chose to find joy in his difficulty, and so can we.

I believe many of us need to pray,

> Father, I'm tired of being a victim and of whining. I'm tired of everybody seeing me in the most pitiful of circumstances.
>
> God, I'm asking You to forgive me and to lift me up.
>
> Father, help me see my circumstances through Your eyes and to begin to see the possibilities, to begin to see the ways in which You have been faithful, and to begin to get a bigger picture of You than I have ever had before.
>
> And Lord, I know that You are sufficient to sustain me, to bless me, and to use me for Your honor and glory.
>
> By your grace, I surrender myself, in my circumstances, to Your will and glory.

That is a prayer of faith! That is the prayer of someone who expects God to be right there in the midst of the storm! And that can be your prayer.

## Take action

Now is always the time to take action.

- Learn to look at your circumstances from God's eyes

- Surrender yourself to God's purposes

- Choose to act instead of react

- Be secure in God

- Walk in the grace that God provides

# CHAPTER 4

# The Joy in Unity

A few years ago, I called a fishing lodge in Alaska and told the manager that I wanted to do some fishing, and that our church wanted to start a church in Alaska. He had a few questions for me, mostly wanting to know who we were and what kind of church we were. Once he found out we had a common bond in Jesus as Lord and Savior, he really opened up.

In the off-season, my newfound friend explained that he lived in rural Oregon where, unfortunately, he had to drive about 45 minutes one way to go to church. That really limited the kind of involvement he had in his church.

One day he called excited that he had made friends with the pastor of a little church in his community. He had found a kinship with this pastor and was thrilled with what God was doing. It blessed me to know that he and his wife and two small children were going to have good fellowship there in his community and would be able to do a better job of leading others into the family of faith.

Soon after, there was a flood and the little church was seriously damaged. They had to completely gut the building and redo all the sheetrock, carpet, painting, etc.

During that process, he told me about how God provided and about how they were going to be able to restore the church and make things better than they were before.

Then several days later he called again. I could tell he was discouraged. "What's going on?" I asked.

He replied, "Man, I don't understand it. Our little congregation has been enjoying great fellowship and God's blessing and we've been working together to rebuild the church, but now we're fussing and fighting."

I probed a bit more, "What's causing it?"

"You won't believe it," he answered. "We are fighting over the color of the paint that we're going to use in the building."

I've used the cliché for years — about churches splitting over the color of carpet — but here it was in cold hard reality!

> There is joy to be found in church fellowship.

My friend was devastated and heartsick at seeing people in his church fighting and divided over what color of paint should go on the walls. Their community desperately needed a positive, radiant witness of Jesus, not a group of squabbling people arguing about irrelevant things.

## Heartbreak is too common

Are you a casualty? Are you a statistic? Have you experienced heartbreak as a result of a similar church experience?

- Have you gone through a church split?

- Have you been wounded by church fights?

- Has your image of church been twisted because of leaders who have fought over the little things?

- Have you dreaded meetings because you knew that the power groups where going to show up and fight, no matter what the issue?

And all of this is within the four walls of a church! This doesn't even count the heartache that is continually being experienced at work, in families, among friends, with relatives, and more.

If anyone should know the joy of unity, it should be those within the family of faith.

## Joy in unity

Paul wrote about the joy that comes from unity when he wrote:

> *Only conduct yourselves in a manner worthy of the gospel of Christ; so that whether I come and see you or remain absent, I will hear of you that you are standing firm in one spirit, with one mind striving together for the faith of the gospel;* (1:27)

What would Paul have said about the church in Oregon arguing about the color of the paint? That couldn't count as acting in a "manner worthy of the gospel of Christ" by any stretch of the imagination!

> *... in no way alarmed by your opponents — which is a sign of destruction for them, but of salvation for you, and that too, from God. For to you it has been granted for Christ's sake, not only to believe in Him, but also to suffer for His sake, experiencing the same conflict which you saw in me, and now hear to be in me* (1:28-30).

The persecution that Paul is talking about comes from outside the church, not from within it.

> *Therefore if there is any encouragement in Christ, if there is any consolation of love, if there is any fellowship of the Spirit, if any affection and compassion, make my joy complete by being of the same mind, maintaining the same love, united in spirit, intent on one purpose* (2:1-2).

Now that is unity!

> *Do nothing from selfishness or empty conceit, but with humility of mind let each of you regard one another as more important than yourselves; do not merely look out for your own personal interests, but also for the interests of others* (2:3-4).

This sounds like a very strong team, operating as one unit with humility and sacrifice. Imagine if we lived in such unity!

## There is power in unity

We all like the benefits of unity, and rightly so, but I believe unity goes a whole lot further than the lack of fighting. There is amazing power that comes to us in our personal lives and in our church fellowship when we are united.

> There is great power in unity.

Only twice does Paul challenge us to walk in a manner that is worthy of the gospel of Christ. What was the context of those challenges?

- It was not with regard to sexual purity.

- It was not with regard to stewardship.

- It was not with regard to living by faith.

Rather, it is with regard to unity.

Paul takes unity very seriously, as should we all. I believe it is consistent with the scriptures to say that it is impossible for you to walk in a manner worthy of the gospel of Jesus Christ if you are not in a united relationship with brothers and sisters!

## #1 — Power through a clear conscience

In Ephesians, Paul also wrote:

> *Therefore, I, the prisoner of the Lord, implore you to walk in a manner worthy of the calling with which you have been called, with all humility and gentleness, with patience, showing tolerance to one another in love, being diligent to preserve the unity of the Spirit in the bond of peace* (4:1-3).

When you know in your heart that you are not allowing anything to divide you from the family of God, **don't you feel good?**

When you are not allowing anything to supersede your commitment to the cause of Christ, **doesn't that excite you?**

When you are making yourself available to be used by God in worship, as a witness, and as a servant to the world around you, **doesn't that light your fire?**

That is the power of a clear conscience! There is power in knowing that we are walking in a manner worthy of the calling that God has given to us.

And we are to remain in that power of a clear conscience.

## #2 — Power of resolve

There is also the power of resolve, which Paul seems to define as: "standing firm in one spirit, with one mind striving together for the faith of the gospel; in no way alarmed by your opponents" (1:27-28).

> Nothing can divide me from the family of God.

You feel the power of resolve when you are standing firm in your spirit, having the sense that together we stand, divided we fall. Add to that the knowledge that God has called us together and that we are committed to one another to uniquely be the body, the voice, and the message of Christ to a lost world, our power goes up several notches!

When we have this power, we don't fear the opposition. The strength of our testimony and the strength of our resolve becomes that wonderful witness to a lost world that there is something here that bears a closer look.

In one of the *Peanuts* comic strips, Lucy demands that Linus change the TV channel, and she threatens him with her fist.

"Well, what makes you think you can walk right in here and take over?" asks Linus.

"These five fingers," says Lucy. "Individually they are nothing, but when I curl them like this into a single unit they form a weapon that is terrible to behold."

"Which channel do you want?" asks Linus. Turning away he looks at his fingers and says, "Why can't you guys get organized like that?"

We Christians should have the power of resolve!

## #3 — Power of team effort

When we use the word "striving," we typically think of difficulty, opposition, and antagonism. But Paul puts two words in combination that changed the meaning altogether. He said that he wanted to hear that the church was *striving together*."

Those are strong, positive, constructive words.

To me, the absolute best picture of "striving together" is watching eight Olympic athletes rowing their sleek boat in perfect unison. They are all on beat, in sync, and rowing together. They are pulling as one in their effort to win the race and it's simply beautiful to see!

That is how the church should be as we strive together.

In the book of Acts, we read how the church was striving together: they were all in one accord, together in one place, the Spirit of God descended on them empowering them and equipping them, they took the message of Jesus to a lost world, and they kept feeling a sense of awe because of what God was doing in their presence.

> Striving isn't the same as strife

Clearly, they were experiencing the power of a team effort! We love it, and God delights in it. I believe it is God's desire to pour this power out on us when our eyes are on Him and our commitment is to work together for His glory.

## Benefits of unity

Are there benefits of walking together in unity? You bet there are. In fact, they are limitless!

I will point out just three of these benefits.

## Benefit #1 — We bless those who observe us

Paul said, "*I want to hear of you ...*" (1:27, emphasis mine). He wanted to know that when people talked about the church, they would be talking about what an amazingly united group of people they were.

The gossip columns should be positive, not negative. Sadly, much of what people say about a church is not positive, is it?

The talk is often about hurt feelings, church splits, someone getting fired, or embarrassing business meetings that took place. Instead, what you should overhear is talk about the church being united, reaching the needy, and impacting the world for Christ.

> God wants to pour out on us the power that comes from unity.

Paul was saying, "When I hear about you, I want it to be the good stuff. I want it to be a testimony that absolutely radiates the presence of Jesus."

A few verses later, Paul writes, "*Make my joy complete by being of the same mind, maintaining the same love, united in spirit, intent on one purpose*" (2:2).

That's a pretty big statement. Of all the things that Paul might have said that would bring joy to his life, it was the prospect of hearing that the church was unified. That would make his joy complete. He wanted to hear that they were standing together, united in heart, with a singleness for their love for God and their purpose for the Lord.

That would bring joy! My hope and prayer is to make this a reality.

## Benefit #2 — You get the best of godly relationships

Paul said, "*I want to hear of you **that you are standing firm in one spirit** ...*" (1:27, emphasis mine).

When we are working together in one spirit, we are unified, and that opens the door to the best of godly relationships. It is the climate or environment where everything flourishes. When we are unified:

- We trust each other.

- We are open with each other.

- We are willing to serve each other.

- We are not worried about ourselves.

- We are not worried about people gossiping.

- We are not worried about people misusing the information we share.

- We know others have our best interest at heart.

- We feel we are bonded together.

- We feel the circle of our fellowship and friendship is growing instead of shrinking.

- We are not hiding behind the barriers of a divided fellowship.

- We are focused.

THAT is what you want!

## Benefit #3 — Your focus is sharp

Paul said, "*I want to hear of you that you are standing firm in one spirit **striving together for the faith of the gospel**" (1:27, emphasis mine).

When you are striving together for one thing, your focus is sharp. You are alert, you are aware, and you are ready to take action. It is with this single-minded focus that Paul challenges the church to take the gospel to the world.

We are to share that same focus.

Consider what Jesus prayed:

> "*I do not ask on behalf of these alone, but for those also who believe in Me through their word; that they may all be one; even as You, Father, are in Me, and I in You, that they also may be in Us, so that the world may believe that You sent Me. The glory which You have given Me I have given to them; that they may be one, just as We are one*" (John 17:20-22).

In unity we have the glory of God on us. Without unity, we lose our access to God's glory.

Jesus went on to say:

> "*I in them and You in Me, that they may be perfected in unity, so that the world may know that You sent Me, and loved them, even as You have loved Me*" (John 17:23).

It is God's intention that as we come together as the family of God in whatever we are doing — Sunday school class, home group, choral worship preparation, or other — it is that unity that perfects us, that matures us, that develops us, and that helps us get the bigger picture of who we are as the people of God.

Great good comes when we are focused.

## Overcoming what threatens our unity

I would not deny for a minute that there are threats to the fellowship from the outside. Worldly influences have a powerfully devastating, undermining affect on churches throughout the world. The enemy is real and the opponents are numerous. There are those who would like to relegate the church to something that is totally insignificant.

However, I believe the greatest threat to our unity is always from within.

### Threat #1 from within — Self-centeredness

Paul warned, *"Do nothing from selfishness or empty conceit ..."* (2:3). That is because he knew that self-centeredness is a cancer that eats away at unity.

> "Complete self-confidence is not only a sin, it's a weakness."
> — G. K. Chesterton

We must maintain the posture and the belief that we desperately need God and each other to accomplish His will on the earth. Dying to self does not mean we become a doormat. Rather, we recognize our need and our value as we joyfully come together.

### Threat #2 from within — Pride

When we have an inflated view of our own self-worth, we become arrogant and proud. We think we have the answers, we know the way to do things, and that our way is the right way, the only way.

> In unity we have the glory of God on us.

As a result, we do not value, much less recognize the unique contribution and unique way God has gifted every other person in God's family. When we fail to value their opinion, we lose the chance to learn, gain, and benefit from them, and everyone is hurt.

Paul gave us the answer when he said, "... *but with humility of mind let each of you regard one another as more important than himself*" (2:3).

I've heard it said that humility is being known for who you are, nothing more and nothing less. When we value others, we all win.

## Threat #3 from within — Failing to fish

I believe the greatest single threat to our unity is the failure to fish. Let me explain.

Author Max Lucado tells a great story of how he once went fishing with his dad and a good friend, Mark. They arrived at their campsite at night and set up their camper, anticipating a glorious day of fishing. However, the next day was too cold and windy to fish, so they stayed inside and played Monopoly and read books. Their spirits were high as they looked forward to the following day.

But the second day was even worse, and tension inside the camper began to build. Mark was beginning to get on Max's nerves, and Max's dad was getting grumpy.

Unfortunately, on the third morning came sleeting rain, and the criticism turned into bickering and fighting. They finally called it quits and headed home in defeat.

Max notes, "I learned a hard lesson that week. Not about fishing, but about people."

And here are the words that apply to every single one of us Christians. Max adds, "**When those who are called to fish don't fish, they fight.**"

Wow!

We are supposed to be fishers of men, as Jesus commanded, but when we are not fishing, it is so easy to start fighting.

Sadly, the following is more true than we would like to admit:

- We throw stones instead of throwing nets.

- We point fingers instead of lending a hand.

- We criticize instead of encouraging.

- We see the faults in others instead of working on our own inefficiencies.

- We believe the worst instead of believing the best.

- We choose to be legalistic instead of obeying God's Word.

But that is not the way it should be, nor is it the way it needs to be. The answer is simple: go fishing. That is because when we fish, we flourish!

- **When we work together, we use the stones for building instead of for throwing.**

- **When we fish together, we lend a hand instead of pointing fingers.**

- **When we are focused on a project together, we encourage our teammates instead of criticizing them.**

- **When we reach out to the needy together, we appreciate each other's gifts instead of critiquing them.**

- **When we face a common task together, we believe the best in our team instead of believing the worst.**

- **When we take the message of Jesus to the lost, we look to Him for real answers instead of relying on old legalistic rules.**

That is the beauty of fishing! When you fish, you flourish.

## The path to unity

Paul said we should be *"united in spirit"* (2:2), but if we try to make the effort to unite ourselves to one another, we are always going to fall flat. There will always be some sense of injustice, some sense of inequity that will surface.

That is why Paul wrote, *"united in spirit, **intent on one purpose**"* (2:2, emphasis mine).

We must be intent on one purpose before we will be united in spirit. That's just the way it works. When we look to Jesus to be our focus, the One by which we line up, the One whom we obey, and when we allow the Spirit of the Living God to be the One to unite our hearts together for His cause and His purpose, there is blessing, there is power, there is victory, and there is unity!

> When those who are called to fish don't fish, they fight. But when they do, they flourish!

As you walk toward unity and the joy that comes through unity, consider these final words:

**Forego**: Do you need to forego the arguing, the complaints, the criticism, and the past history of disappointments you've held on to for a very long time? If so, let it go.

**Forgive**: Do you need to forgive others within the church who have hurt you, whether intentionally or unintentionally, so you can be free? If so, let go. Forgive them. Euodia and Syntyche will forever be known (Philippians 4:2) for their fussing and fighting. Nobody wants to be remembered for that. God is calling us to forgive, experience His grace, and move on.

**Focus**: Do you focus on loving Jesus and loving others? This lifts all of us out of the mundane, out of the distractions of the world.

**Fish**: Do you go fishing? Find your place on the fishing team. I'm a fisherman and I love to fish; but, let me tell you, there is no greater joy than being able to cast the net and see lost people come to faith in Christ. That's what God has called us to be about.

May you find great pleasure in the joy that comes from unity!

## Take action

- Now is always the time to take action.

- You have power in a clear conscience, in resolve, and in team effort.

- Bless those who observe you.

- Overcome self-centeredness by loving others.

- Beat pride by choosing humility.

- Stop fighting by fishing.

CHAPTER 5

# The Joy of a
# Good Attitude

I have enjoyed good health all my life. I was a senior in high school before I ever missed a day of school because of illness, but when we as a church were on a mission trip to the Philippines, I got hit hard by the stomach bug, "Montezuma's revenge," as many call it.

We had a church full of Filipinos who had come to hear this American preach, and I didn't feel as though I could let them down. But I told the pastor I might have to run out the door, and he would need to take over at that point. As I preached, sweat was dripping off my body and my stomach was just screaming for me to get out of there!

I made it through the message and got to the invitation and turned to the pastor who was translating and said, "You need to give the invitation."

He turned back to me and said, "No, no. You give the invitation." I wanted to say, "You don't understand! I can't stand here for another second," but I went ahead and gave the invitation. The whole time I was thinking, "This is not going to be pretty."

We finally got to the end of the invitation, and I made a dash for the door. Well, I'm about 6'4" and that puts me, on average, a full 12" taller than Filipino people ... and doorways in Filipino houses.

> You can have a good attitude in spite of adversity and difficulty.

I cracked my head on the doorway as I ran out. Bam! I thought to myself, "God, just kill me now!"

But I survived it and God showed Himself mighty through our time in the Philippines.

As I was thinking about that predicament, the Lord reminded me of Pastor Mack Cole. Mack and his wife, Carol, pastor the Big Horn Baptist Church in Fort Smith, Montana. It's a little bitty community at the end of the road. You will never drive through Fort Smith; you have to go there. He is 81 years old and has terrible, debilitating rheumatoid arthritis. But theirs is the only church in that community.

And every Sunday morning he gets up at a very early hour to begin the painful, laborious process of getting himself ready. Then Carol drives him over the short distance to the church, gets him in his wheel chair and helps him get behind the pulpit an hour before the service starts so he can compose himself and recover.

Then when the service begins, he leads the worship and preaches the message to the handful of people who are there.

I think about Mack Cole and Carol demonstrating that powerful witness of a good attitude in spite of such adversity and such difficulty. They have a great attitude, which brings them joy and inspires and blesses others.

## Your good attitude affects you

Did you see the *Peanuts* comic where Lucy asked Charlie Brown, "Did you ever know anyone who was really happy?"

Just then, Snoopy came dancing into the next frame, nose up in the air, dancing as only Snoopy can, and he dances away across the frame as Lucy and Charlie watch in amazement.

In the last frame, Lucy finishes her question: "Did you ever know anyone who was really happy **who was in his right mind**?"

Funny, and true in many ways. We choose our attitude, and though others may think we are strange, it affects us in a very good way.

With this in mind, consider what Jesus said: "*I have come that you might have life, and that you might have it more abundantly*" (John 10:10).

> "I am come that you might have life, and that you might have it more abundantly."
> – Jesus

We know that Jesus came to save us from our sins, but I think that He also came to save us from ourselves.

His plan is that we have abundant life, and many times He needs to rescue us from the bad attitudes, the victim mentality, and the cynicism that seem to permeate the world in which we live.

I believe these words of Jesus are the foundation of our good attitude.

## Paul's example of joy through a good attitude

Paul is a great example of someone who has joy through a good attitude. He challenged us to do the same when he wrote:

> *Have this attitude in yourselves which was also in Christ Jesus, who, although He existed in the form of God, did not regard equality with God a thing to be grasped, but He emptied Himself, taking the form of a bondservant, and being made in the likeness of men* (2:5-7).

Jesus had the right attitude, and that is the attitude we are to mirror.

*Being found in appearance as a man, He humbled Himself by becoming obedient to the point of death, even death on a cross. For this reason also, God highly exalted Him, and bestowed on Him the name which is above every name, so that at the name of Jesus every knee will bow, of those who are in heaven and on earth and under the earth, and that every tongue will confess that Jesus Christ is Lord, to the glory of God the Father (2:8-11).*

Jesus chose humility and obedience, and then accomplished God's will. We are to also do the same.

*So then, my beloved, just as you have always obeyed, not as in my presence only, but now much more so in my absence, work out your salvation with fear and trembling; for it is God who is at work in you, both to will and to work for His good pleasure (2:12-13).*

I love this part! God is at work in your life and my life to accomplish His will. This is an attitude boost if I've ever seen one.

*Do all things without grumbling or disputing; so that you may prove yourselves to be blameless and innocent, children of God above reproach in the midst of a crooked and perverse generation, among whom you appear as lights in the world, holding fast the word of life, so that in the day of Christ I will have reason to glory because I did not run in vain nor toil in vain (2:14-16).*

Like water to fire is grumbling to a good attitude! It kills it faster than it takes to read this sentence. When we free ourselves from disputing and discord, even our attitude can be a light to the world for Jesus.

*But even if I am being poured out as a drink offering upon the sacrifice and service of your faith, I rejoice and share my joy with you all. You too, I urge you, rejoice in the same way and share your joy with me* (2:17-18).

Paul had made the choice that no matter what happened to him he would rejoice and have joy to spare!

How can we go about getting that same positive attitude?

## Step #1 to building a good attitude

A good attitude originates with God. Paul challenges us to have the attitude that Jesus had.

I don't know about you, but that is pretty intimidating. Paul is not simply suggesting that we have a sweet spirit or that we have an optimistic outlook on life. Instead, he is saying that we also need to be willing to:

- humble ourselves

- give up what is rightfully ours for the needs of others

- be obedient to the will of the Father

- express a sacrificial kind of love

That is a lot to ask, and we simply cannot do it in our own strength, which is why Paul said that Jesus is our example.

> A good attitude originates with God.

What this means for us is that we must acknowledge that a good attitude isn't something we manufacture, it isn't something we're simply born with, and it isn't something we're able to conjure up on a good day.

In Romans, Paul says:

> *Therefore, I urge you, brethren, by the mercies of God, to present your bodies a living and holy sacrifice, acceptable to God, which is your spiritual service of worship. And do not be conformed to the world, but be transformed by the renewing of your mind ...* (12:1-2).

But the world mindset that affects all of us and continually speaks into our ears, says:

- **Stand up for your rights.**

- **Get what is yours.**

- **If you can't win, take them to court.**

- **And if someone offends you, complain, gripe, and moan.**

But Paul challenges us to recognize that when we come to faith in Christ there is a power that makes it possible for our mind and our whole outlook to be truly transformed.

In 2 Corinthians he says almost the same thing:

> *If any one is in Christ, he is a new creation; the old things passed away; behold, new things have come* (5:17).

Everything — our outlook, our attitude, the way we see circumstances, and the way we look at those closest to us — now has the potential of being seen through the eyes of Jesus and taking on a totally new meaning.

I am convinced that it is God's desire that you have a good attitude, a healthy outlook, a positive disposition that embraces life, celebrates each day, and is convinced God is

> Come to faith in Christ for your whole outlook to be transformed.

at work in your life for His glory. It is God's desire and gift to you.

## Step #2 to building a good attitude

Some people were born into families where good attitudes and sunny dispositions were modeled; but, most of us weren't so fortunate. We saw or experienced not the best of attitudes and knew deep down that there had to be a better way. There had to be more!

But whether we had good examples or not, if we really want to have the mind of Christ, if we want to have the attitude of Jesus, it requires something very, very important that we must give of ourselves to accomplish.

A good attitude requires self-discipline.

Look at what Paul wrote:

> *So then, my beloved, just as you have always obeyed, not as in my presence only, but now much more so in my absence, work out your salvation with fear and trembling ... Do all things without grumbling or disputing* (2:12, 14).

Author John Ortberg, in his book *The Life You Always Wanted*, gave a great imaginary example of a couch potato who was unexpectedly selected to run a marathon.

Though the couch potato dreamed of being an elite athlete, winning the gold medal, and basking in the praise of the world, the couch potato knew that he couldn't possibly run a marathon.

No matter how strong the desire and no matter how much he really, really wanted to win, the couch potato knew that it would take a change in routine, a change in eating habits, a change in exercise habits, a change in thinking, and a change of focus.

> A good attitude originates with God, but it requires self-discipline.

Trying wouldn't cut it. To win, it would require training. And training requires self-discipline.

Similarly, when it comes to having a good attitude, when it comes to our embracing a life that Christ offers to us, it requires more than simply trying. It involves training.

Paul says we are to *"work out"* our salvation. Is he saying that we have to earn our salvation? Not at all! There is nothing you can do to earn your salvation, for salvation is a gift from God, but this does not negate the fact that you have to work.

> When we rise to the level of joy that is available to us as the gift of God, it makes it possible for us to make an impact on our lost world in a way that nothing else can.

Paul goes on to say that *"it is God who is at work in you, both to will and to work for His good pleasure"* (2:13). The challenge is for us to live our life in a way that allows what Christ has made possible in us to come to fruition and to be made manifest in all of the things we do.

It is as if Paul knows our tendencies. He goes on to say that it is important to go about this without grumbling and complaining. Author Scott Peck, in his book *The Road Less Traveled*, wisely noted:

Life is difficult. This is a great truth ... one of the greatest truths. It is a great truth because once we truly see this truth, we transcend it. Most people don't truly see this truth — that life is difficult. Instead, they moan, more or less incessantly, noisily, or subtlety about the enormity of their problems, their burdens, their difficulties as if life were generally easy, as if life should be easy. They voice their belief, again noisily or sometimes subtly, that their difficulties somehow are a unique kind of affliction that should not be. And that has somehow been visited upon them, or their family, or their tribe, or their class, or their nation, or their race, but not upon others.

Tim Hansel, in his book *You've Got to Keep Dancing,* wrote the following:

Pain is inevitable, but misery is optional. We cannot avoid pain, but we can avoid joy. God has given us such immense freedom that He will allow us to be as miserable as we want to be. Joy is simple, not to be confused with easy. At any moment in life, we have at least two options and one of them is to choose an attitude, a posture of grace, a commitment to joy.

I know that a lot of people were not merely touched by the bad they had experienced. In many cases, they were scarred by the bad attitudes of their home life, work environment, or school situation. Angry, vindictive, cynical people can leave such pain in their wake that it's almost beyond comprehension!

> "Life is difficult. This is a great truth. One of the greatest truths. It is a great truth because once we truly see this truth, we transcend it."
> — Scott Peck

But God has something more positive for us than the negatives that we've experienced. It is God's

69

will for us who bear His name to be the very people who are making the positive impact on negatives of this world, and doing so in a way that God gets the credit for it.

We are to take the very attitude, the very mindset of Jesus that changed our lives and allow the Spirit of Christ to work through us in such a way that truly it becomes the means by which others come to know Jesus as Lord and Savior.

I love the language Paul uses here. He says, "... *prove yourselves to be blameless* ..." (2:15). It's not enough for us to say we are Christians. It is not enough for us to say we know that Jesus lifts us and helps overcome the negative attitude of the world, the victim mentality; but, Paul is saying we should be the very proof everywhere we go.

> "Pain is inevitable, but misery is optional. We cannot avoid pain, but we can avoid joy."
> — Tim Hansel

In all likelihood, the most difficult place for us to do this is in our homes, at our workplaces, and in our classrooms. But the power of God is able to work out our salvation even in the most difficult of circumstances.

I challenge you by the grace that God has given you to prove to the world that Christ really has made a difference in your life. He says we are to be children of God above reproach, and for us to have the reputation that there is something wonderful, something special about us.

And you can through His power.

## Like a moth to a flame, joy attracts the lost

There are two streams of evangelistic effort. In the first, we go out and present the plan of salvation, conduct crusades, and send missionaries to the far corners of the world.

In the second, we attract people to Jesus by being who Christ makes it possible for us to be. As a result, the lost sit up and take notice and say:

- I want what you have.

- I want the peace, joy, and hope that I see in you.

- I see how you face difficulty and how you face adversity.

- I want to know the secret you seem to have found that has made such a profound difference in your life.

Paul said that you are to be a light in the world. So, whether you are involved in the first or the second method of evangelism, recognize that when you allow the Holy Spirit of God to produce that gift of joy in your life, you light up the world around you.

> **It is God's will for us to make a difference in our world.**

There is such an amazing contrast between you and those around you that it cannot be denied.

It goes without saying that we are drawn to people with good attitudes and to people who have a positive spirit. They are able to refresh us, to encourage us, to bless us and to lift us up. And their good attitude is contagious.

By the same token, when we are around negative people, it is amazing how quickly we deteriorate into that negative spirit, how we begin to get grumpy, and how nothing seems to satisfy us.

Paul says:

> *Even if I am being poured out as a drink offering upon the sacrifice and service of your faith, I rejoice and share my joy with you all* (2:17).

Paul is saying all this from a prison cell. His future is uncertain and it may cost him his life. Yet, in all of this, he counts it all joy and would do it over again!

What do you think the impact of his words had on the readers of his day? I imagine it caused them to look at their circumstances in a whole new light. I suspect in some ways his words even shamed them. No doubt it stopped the grumbling and disputing over little insignificant things.

Also, I'm sure many prayed, "Lord, help me get the big picture of what life is all about. Help me be like Paul."

Paul's attitude was attractive, and it rubbed off on everyone who came in contact with him.

## Your attitude is a choice

When it comes right down to it, your attitude is a choice. Paul reminds us of this fact when he wrote, *"You too, I urge you, rejoice in the same way and share your joy with me"* (2:18).

The only way you can rejoice in the same way and share the same joy is if you have chosen to have a good attitude, chosen to let God work that positive attitude into your life, and chosen to be self-disciplined.

> Spread it around! There is something amazingly contagious about a good attitude and a joyous spirit.

It begins with your choice. Then God helps you each step of the way.

When you are plugged into a group of believers, you are in the right place, ready to grow, to mature, and to be the light. Bible study classes, discipleship groups, and all of the other ministry opportunities have a two-fold purpose: God works through you and God works in you.

As God works through you, lives are impacted. A good friend of mine, Paul J. Meyer, wrote a powerful book on the topic of forgiveness. He regularly receives letters, faxes, and emails of how lives have been changed as a result of the book. God worked through him in a mighty way.

God also works in you as you work together with other believers. Something powerful happens when we get brothers and sisters in Christ together, when we begin to share the journey and when we begin to share the joy of knowing we are in the will of God. The goal is evident, and we know there is a purpose for our lives.

> Rejoice and share your joy with others.

And living like this, Paul would say, brings great joy in his heart, your heart, and God's heart.

Simply put, choose today to have a good attitude.

## Take action

- Now is always the time to take action.

- Ask God to give you the same attitude that was in Jesus.

- Choose to be self-disciplined.

- Let God's light shine through you.

- Go fishing.

# CHAPTER 6

# Life's Greatest Joy

Joy is available to us all, regardless of our circumstances or how we feel. As we zero in on God's Word, mining, as it were, the truths in the Bible, it is amazing to see the joy that is available to us as followers of Jesus.

Not only is it available, but it is God's desire that we abide in His joy, and that we experience it continually.

> God wants you to have consistent, abiding joy.

As you know, Paul wrote the letter of Philippians from prison, and right in the middle of his letter, he felt compelled to share his testimony.

Why? Because it was through his testimony that Paul could tell about life's greatest joy.

## Rejoice in the Lord

Paul wrote:

> *Finally, my brethren, rejoice in the Lord. To write the same things again is no trouble to me, and it is a safeguard for you* (Philippians 3:1).

These words refocus us as followers of Jesus on one thing: rejoicing in the Lord. If you want the characteristic outlook that God desires for your daily routine, your daily life, and your daily attitude, here it is in a nutshell.

When you wake up in the morning and go through the day, when you spend time with your family, as you lay your head on the pillow, it is God's will that you be filled with His wonderful joy.

We can't go wrong in hearing this encouragement again. In fact, one of the best ways to teach something is to tell your students what you are going to tell them, then tell them, and then tell them what you told them. You present it three times, which drives home the point. Paul has effectively done the same with us.

## Beware of dogs

Paul wrote:

> Beware of the dogs ... (3:2).

Obviously, Paul is not talking of Lassie and Old Yeller. He's not talking about the household pets that we love and cherish and probably spend way too much money on.

Not at all. Paul is warning us about the people who want to rob you of your joy, undermine your joy, enslave you, and absolutely gut you of any real, lasting joy that you might have experienced.

It is horrific, and he's painting a very vivid picture of roving hoards of dogs, mongrels that were out on their own in the streets of that day. These dogs fed on refuse, even on the young and the weak, and would steal anything they could. But it's what dogs do.

> Watch out for those who want to rob you of your joy.

I've had dogs most of my life. I've had bird dogs, and I've always fed them well; but, it was amazing to me when we would go hunting and they would come on some dead carcass that was there for who knows how long, they would lunch on it like it was prime rib. I'm trying to keep them from wallowing in it, eating it, and rolling in it, but they were invariably drawn to it!

Dogs are simply drawn to dead, rotten things, but a pack of wild hungry dogs will not wait for things to die. They will hunt and kill, so the warning is to be taken seriously.

There are some dogs that I am just automatically cautious around, such as a Doberman Pincher, a German Shepherd, or a Rottweiller. I want to give them a wide berth, knowing full well that they could hurt me. But the fact is, I've never been bitten by one of these breeds.

You know the kind of dog that has bitten me more often than not? It's the dag-gone Chihuahua! I can't tell you how many times some old lady would be holding a cute little puppy, and I would reach out to pet it, and it will bite my finger off!

Interestingly, the danger of these little dogs is not always obvious. Similarly, sometimes the people who seem so cute and cuddly are the ones who have lost the joy, lost the direction, and lost the perspective in their own lives. All they know to do is snarl and snap and bite those around them.

> **Evil workers have lost sight of Jesus.**

We are warned — avoid the dogs!

## Beware of evil workers

Paul wrote:

> ... *beware of the evil workers* ... (3:2).

Who are these evil workers Paul is talking about? Satanists? Pagans? No, he is talking about people who go in the name of Christianity.

He's talking about those who, perhaps at one point in their lives, really did line up under true Biblical authority, who really did understand the liberation they experienced as a follower of Jesus, but not any more.

These "evil workers" lost sight of Jesus in their own personal lives, and ended up being used by Satan to affect the family of faith. They work to undermine the joy and the confidence and the optimistic spirit the Lord wants the church to have. And lastly, they are constantly calling our attention away from Jesus as Lord.

> Avoid those who don't lift you up, energize you, or set you free.

If you find yourself in the company of "evil workers," recognize that their intentions don't match yours in the slightest. Get out of that relationship as fast as you can!

## Beware of false circumcision

Paul wrote:

> ... *beware of the false circumcision* ... (3:2).

This warning was very relevant to those who were impacted by Paul's teachings. Every time he started a church, there would be people who would come behind him and say:

- Paul has only preached part of the gospel to you.

- If you want to be rightly related with God, then what he has taught you is not enough.

- You've got to become a full-fledged Jew.

- You've got to go through all the things that make you a Jew before you will ultimately be acceptable to God.

Rules and religion at its finest! Paul said these people were the "false circumcision" because of their efforts to do things in the flesh, to focus on the outside and not deal with real issues on the inside. Through external effort, the "false circumcision" preached a message of rules and religion to gain acceptance by God.

> We are to worship in the Spirit of God and we are to glory in Christ Jesus.

You see, most of the world's religions buy into the notion that you have to work your way to heaven. No God would simply love and accept you, they reason, so you have to earn the right for God to accept and love you … and that love is always conditional. Hope of heaven is always a little uncertain, but that is part of it.

Talk about hopeless! And that is why Paul warns against those who preach the false circumcision.

Later, in 2 Timothy 3, Paul describes these "false circumcision" people in more detail: they look godly, they look spiritual, and they sound religious; but, they have no power of God in their lives. They are of no help to you, they cannot set you free, and they do not have joy. Paul's encouragement: avoid people like these.

In evangelical Christianity there will, every once in a while, come a fad that countless churches embrace. Maybe the fad is centered on a book or workbook or seminar; but, if you listen closely, you will see the legalistic aspects behind it.

The legalistic element says that if you are not following Jesus exactly the way we are prescribing it, then you are not quite right with God, you are not fully there, you are not good enough, etc.

Ultimately, the legalism entraps you and takes your eyes off the sufficiency of Jesus, the sufficiency of grace that reveals the difference between legalism and freedom, life and death.

Watch out for the false circumcision!

## We are the true witnesses

Paul continued:

> ... *for we are the true circumcision, who worship in the Spirit of God and glory in Christ Jesus* ... (3:3).

Quite overtly, Paul said that some outside influences (dogs, evil workers, false circumcision) would love to steal your joy. Now on a more subtle level, he shifts the focus away from the outward threats and on to the threats-that come from within.

Paul reminded his readers that they were the true circumcision who had allowed the inside — their hearts — to be changed, and as a result had become new people because they experienced the grace of God that set them free.

He also reminds us what it ought to look like to be a person filled with joy following Jesus. He says we are to worship in the Spirit of God, and we are to glory in Christ Jesus.

That is pretty basic, isn't it? That's pretty straightforward. I'm convinced the longer I live that it should be the goal of every one of us to simplify our lives. Paul, I think, was trying to remind his readers to keep it simple.

Remember what the basic elements of this life are all about:

- It is worshiping in the Spirit.

- It is allowing a freedom in your heart that says, "I want to embrace God. I want my life to be identified with Him. I want everything I do to bring honor and glory to the name of Jesus."

- It is to point people to Christ.

- It is to unashamedly say, "Whoever I am, whatever value and benefit you see in my life, it is all because of Jesus and nothing of who I am."

## No hope in yourself

Paul outlined in great detail:

> ... *put no confidence in the flesh, although I myself might have confidence even in the flesh. If anyone else has a mind to put confidence in the flesh, I far more: circumcised the eighth day, of the nation of Israel, of the tribe of Benjamin, a Hebrew of Hebrews; as to the Law, a Pharisee; as to zeal, a persecutor of the church; as to the righteousness which is in the Law, found blameless* (3:3-6).

Without question, Paul was the epitome of the perfect Jew. He had all the credentials, the proper upbringing, all the awards, and a track record to prove it all. No doubt he was on the Who's Who list back then, but Paul would not put an ounce of confidence in any of it.

Why? Because Paul knew the truth.

The dogs, evil workers, and false circumcision people tried to cover it up, to pretend it wasn't there, but Paul kept coming back to the truth: Jesus.

> Our hope is only in Jesus.

In spite of all Paul's zeal, study, and upbringing, without Jesus, he could not be right with God. Paul knew this, and fully embraced it. That was the only way to fill his deep hunger for God, the deep hole in his heart and in his life that had never been satisfied.

Paul had no hope in himself. Instead, he found hope in Jesus.

Tim Keller, in his book *The Reason For God*, sheds some light on what happens when we look to anything other than God:

> Sin isn't only doing bad things. It is more fundamentally making good things into ultimate things. Sin is building your life and meaning on anything, even a good thing, more than on God. Whatever we build our life on will drive us and enslave us. Sin is primarily idolatry.

What this means to you and me, Tim Keller explains, may surprise us. He goes on to state:

- If you center your life on your spouse or partner, you will be emotionally dependent, jealous, controlling. The other person's problems will be overwhelming to you.

- If you center your life on your family and children, you will try to live your life through your children until they resent you or have no self of their own. At worst you may abuse them when they displease you.

- If you center your life and identity on your work and career, you will be a driven workaholic, a boring, shallow person. At worst you will lose family and friends, and, if your career goes poorly, you will develop deep depression.

- If you center your life and identity on money and possessions, you will be eaten up by worry or jealousy about money. You'll be willing to do unethical things to maintain your lifestyle, which will eventually blow up your life.

- If you center your life and identity on pleasure, gratification, or comfort, you will find yourself getting addicted to something. You will become chained to the escape strategies by which you avoid the hardness of life.

- If you center your life and identity on relationships and approval, you will be constantly hurt by criticism and thus always losing friends. You will fear confronting others; and, therefore, will be a useless friend.

- If you center your life and your identity on a noble cause, you will divide the world into good and bad and demonize your opponents. Ironically, you will be controlled by your enemies. Without them, you will have no purpose.

- If you center your life and your identity on religion and morality, you will (if you're living up to your moral standards) be proud, self-righteous, and cruel. If you don't live up to your moral standards, your guilt will be utterly devastating.

Without question, Paul knew exactly what he was saying when he said he had no hope in himself.

## None of it counts

Paul wrote:

> *But whatever things were gain to me, those things I have counted as loss for the sake of Christ. More than that, I count all things to be loss in view of the surpassing value of knowing Christ Jesus my Lord, for whom I have suffered the loss of all things, and count them but rubbish so that I may gain Christ, and may be found in Him, not having a righteousness of my own derived from the Law, but that which is*

*through faith in Christ, the righteousness which comes from God on the basis of faith … (3:7-9).*

Plainly, for all to see, Paul freely admits that everything that was important to him, everything that might have made him acceptable to God, doesn't count for anything!

> ## Have you come to the same revelation as Paul?

He uses powerful language. He uses graphic language! He calls it all rubbish, trash, refuse, dung! It is all utterly and completely of no value whatsoever in making himself right with God.

It is only through grace that we can be God's children.

Paul challenges us to understand this for ourselves and not to be duped by anyone into somehow believing that we can add to God's grace, that we can somehow do something that could convince God that He now had to accept us.

None of it counts.

## The power of His resurrection

Paul went on to say:

> *… that I may know Him, and the power of His resurrection and the fellowship of His sufferings, being conformed to His death; in order that I may attain to the resurrection from the dead. Not that I have already obtained it or have already become perfect, but I press on so that I may lay hold of that for which also I was laid hold of by Christ Jesus (3:10-12).*

It is one thing for us to intellectually say we believe Jesus is the Son of God who lived a perfect life, who died on the cross, who was buried, and who rose again, and who is on the right hand of God.

It is one thing for us to intellectually say that we believe all of that.

But Paul said there came a time in his life when that truth moved from simply an intellectual under-standing to a heart-felt, life-changing moment.

> Jesus Christ, who took away the sin of the world, took my sin away.

He realized that Jesus, the Lamb of God who took away the sin of the world, took his sins away. And when he placed his faith in Him, he found that God's power which brought Jesus back from the dead became his power.

As Paul came to that faith conclusion, it brought him life. He became a new person. He was set free from all of the slavery of trying to work his way into God's good graces. He was set free from an impos-sible task of trying to earn his way to heaven. And he found that God gave this powerful invitation to him to come into a life-changing relationship where he could know Him.

As a result, Paul says he gained Christ forever and ever. And not only does he know the power of His resurrection, but he shares this amazing fellowship in times of suffering, and that transforms everything, giving him a perspective he could never have had apart from Jesus.

Truly, Paul was a changed man because of Jesus at work in his life.

## If you lost your joy

If you have lost the joy of your relationship with Jesus, it may have been because of the dogs, the evil workers, the false circumcision legalists, or something else.

Whatever the case, Jesus wants to set you free!

To be free, you will have to give all your hurts, all your frustrations, and all your disappointments over to Him. Tell the Lord, "I want to put my eyes back on you. You alone are Lord. You are sufficient."

And if you are holding on to any thought that what you have done is going to get you into heaven, you need to realize that is absolute garbage, utter rubbish. It counts for nothing. Your hope of eternal life is solely on the basis of God's love for you expressed in Jesus Christ.

And that is life's greatest joy!

## Take action

- Now is always the time to take action.

- Rejoice in the Lord.

- Beware of dogs, evil workers, and false circumcision.

- Remember that it's 0% you and 100% Him.

- Experience the power of His resurrection.

- Get your joy back if you've lost it.

- Claim it if you never have.

# CHAPTER 7

# The Joy of the Journey

If life is a journey, how would you describe yourself on that journey?

Take a second to describe yourself. Are you …

**Rattled?** Have you gone through some unsettling events? From health issues to politics and from the weather to the economy, there are plenty of things happening that may feel like bumps and potholes along the way.

**Scared?** Maybe you don't like what you are seeing or experiencing in your life or in the world around you. It can be scary, that's for sure.

**Lost and needing a map?** It might be that you would describe your journey as a little lost. You're not real sure where you are or how to get where you think you need to go.

**Broken down?** Perhaps you feel as though you are stuck on the side of the road. You aren't going anywhere and are not sure how to get things moving again.

**Speeding and out of control?** Would you say that life is just speeding by way too fast? You feel out of control as you rush pell-mell to some unknown destination. You want to slow down and gain control, but don't know how to do that.

**Enjoying the ride?** Ideally, you have accepted the fact that the journey is demanding, even difficult, but you have chosen to maintain your joy each and every day. You are keeping your faith, hope, and peace placed in Jesus, knowing full well that He is directing your steps.

I hope you are enjoying the ride!

**I know that God has for us, every single one of us** — in spite of circumstances, economics, weather, the price of gasoline, etc. — **joy that He wants us to experience every day along the way on our journey.**

> God has joy that He wants us to experience every day on our journey.

It's ours, if we want it.

Paul had a victorious spirit and went boldly into the unknown that God had for him. Along the way, Paul learned how to have joy in the journey, and he gave us five words of advice that will enable us to do the same.

## Advice #1 — Keep on keeping on

For some, "get going again" may be more accurate, but whatever the case, what matters is that we continue to move forward in our walk with God, that we maintain the course, that we keep going.

Paul wrote:

> *Not that I have already obtained it or have already become perfect, but I press on so that I may lay hold of that for which also I was laid hold of by Jesus Christ (3:12).*

And two verses later he said:

> *I press on toward the goal for the prize of the upward call of God in Christ Jesus (3:14).*

When we talk about getting going or moving forward, the first barrier to overcome is inertia.

Sadly, many of us have set some goals in life, we have made some plans, we've thought about some wonderful vacations or some particular trips that have had appeal to us. We've been talking about them and planning them for years, but we've never made the first move … we've never started on that journey.

> **The first barrier to overcome is inertia.**

Overcoming inertia has to be the biggest challenge in life for all of us when we think about the journey Christ has set before us, that He wants us to experience, and that He wants us to complete.

Each of us must overcome inertia.

I often hear people talking about being tired. Well, I've come to see that there is a good tired and there is a bad tired. A good tired means you are exhausted from working hard, that your muscles are sore because you've paid a price, and that you've given your all to what you are working on.

But, a deep sense of satisfaction accompanies the good tired. What's more, you sleep well and wake up refreshed and rested because you gave yourself to something truly worthwhile.

> **Life is so worthwhile! We all must make the effort to experience it.**

But, there is a bad tired that has a very different kind of effect on you. It's a tired that comes from emptiness, from wondering if there is meaning to what you are doing, from boredom, and from being powerless to bring about any change.

And when it comes to sleeping, the bad tired leaves you feeling just as weary as when you went to sleep. The bad tired leaves you lethargic, sad, and un-inspired. No fun at all!

Twice, Paul says, "I press on." It doesn't require a linguist to picture someone who is fully engaged, who is using all of his strength, all of his energy to move forward in life, wanting to make progress.
We are to press on, and that is exactly how to overcome inertia! We exert our will to take the first, then the second step. Let's get going!

## Advice #2 — Don't camp too long in one place

Paul gave us a very practical warning when he said:

> *Brethren, I do not regard myself as having laid hold of it yet; but one thing I do: forgetting what lies behind and reaching forward to what lies ahead ... (3:13).*

Moses got the direct word from God: "*You have stayed long enough at this mountain*" (Deuteronomy 1:6). At Mount Sinai God had given Moses the Ten Commandments. God was there, the mountain shook, fire and lightning could be seen and heard, and God's presence could be felt. It was a "mountain top" experience to say the least; but, it soon became time to move on. God had many more things for Moses to accomplish.

> God wants you to experience Him in the present tense, not the past tense.

In the New Testament, Peter, James, and John were on a mountain when they saw Jesus being transfigured before them, heard God praise His Son, and witnessed Moses and Elijah standing there talking to Jesus. Peter proposed that they make tabernacles or shelters so that the experience could continue, but that was not Jesus' intent at all.

Mountain top experiences are wonderful, and it's right for us to desire those experiences where we get a new perspective and be refreshed in our spirit ... but you can't live on top of a mountain.

If you find yourself longing to remain or return to a mountain top experience, it's time to let it go and move on. Some people actually need to forget what they have already done for God. In remembering, they coast on their past records, achievements, accomplishments, and mountain top experiences.

Everyone needs to rejoice, honor, and celebrate what God has done in his life, but time doesn't stand still. God wants you to experience Him in the present tense, not the past tense. You are to keep moving forward, accomplishing the next thing that He has for you.

Perhaps you've been tempted to think, "I've already done my part. I've already made my contribution. Now I'm going to take it easy." You must not give into that. Instead, you need to press on, like Paul did, to the next thing that God has for you.

> Forget what's behind you and move forward.

Some people have experienced the opposite of a mountain top experience, but the advice to forget the past and move on is just as relevant.

You may need to draw on God's grace in a fresh and powerful way so you can stop remembering, and be released from your past. Perhaps you need to say:

- Because of what Jesus did on the cross for me, my sin is forgiven.

- Jesus, help me claim what You have already done for me. You have forgiven and forgotten what was held against me.

- Lord, there is some junk, some failures, in my past that I need to be able to let go of. I need to be able to put them behind me so they aren't constantly tripping me up, beating me up, intimidating me, and robbing me of the joy that You have for me.

- Lord, help me receive Your liberating grace.

Whatever it may be that tries to rob you of joy and ruin your future, I believe the Spirit of the Living God would like to speak into your heart and say that you need to forget what's behind. You need to move forward to what God has for you today and tomorrow and the next day.

Like Paul, you press on.

### Advice #3 — Choose your companions very carefully

There are three powerful pieces of advice that Paul gave us when he wrote:

> *Brethren, join in following my example, and observe those who walk according to the pattern you have in us. For many walk, of whom I often told you, and now tell you even weeping, that they are enemies of the cross of Christ ...* (3:17-18).

On life's journey, having the right companions is incredibly important, and Paul knows that. His advice is very clear.

**Follow my example:** Paul could say "follow my example" because he knew the good that would come as we get into the Word of God. He challenged us to join him in the journey of life. No, it would not be about our comfort or our past achievements. It would be about looking day by day for the opportunity to honor Jesus and to do what He called us to do.

That is why Bible study is so important. The time you spend in the Word of God enables you to apply truths to your daily life. In so doing, it unleashes for you the power that is available for you to do what God wants you to do in our world.

**Observe those who live by the same values:** I grew up in a home where my dad never looked for an opportunity to praise anyone. He always looked for the dark, for the failing, and for what he could criticize. I've had to struggle with that, and through the years I've seen there are many guilty of the same thing in churches. We don't need critics — we need encouragers!

Paul says to observe or look for those who share your same heart and passion for the things of Jesus. It goes without saying that we are talking about finding what is positive, what is redeeming, and what is uplifting. And when you find these people, embrace them! It will motivate you to keep moving forward with joy in life.

Those who have a critical spirit are people who have been robbed of joy, robbed of seeing the very best in life, and robbed of seeing God at work in the lives of others around them. Don't go there! And if you need help in this area, ask God to set you free.

**Watch out for enemies of the cross of Christ:** Paul cries when he talks about the enemies of the cross of Christ. He is not smugly telling us to avoid these people. Not at all. Instead, his heart breaks for them because he knows their end is destruction.

You have a decision to make: who is going on the journey of life with you and who is not. You need to be very careful to avoid those people who have set their minds on the things of the world. You need to have discernment as to who those people are, to be able to see the worldliness in their lifestyle, and not to align yourself with them.

## Advice #4 — Keep your destination and your goal clearly in mind

Paul wrote:

> *Our citizenship is in heaven, which also we eagerly wait for a Savior, the Lord Jesus Christ; who will transform the body of our humble state into conformity with the body of His glory, by the exertion of the power that He has to subject all things to Himself* (3:20-21).

The destination, Paul states, is heaven. We have our citizenship there! That is the destination where Christians will ultimately end up. And the goal? Paul says the goal is:

- to *"know Him, and the power of His resurrection and the fellowship of His sufferings ... that I may attain to the resurrection from the dead"* (3:10).

- to *"lay hold of that for which also I was laid hold of by Jesus Christ"* (3:12).

- and *"I press on toward the goal for the prize of the upward call of God in Christ Jesus"* (3:14).

> **Keep your destination clearly in mind.**

Simply put, Jesus is our goal.

Paul is saying that what makes his life tick are the consuming thoughts of knowing Jesus, knowing that Jesus is at work in him, and knowing that Jesus is transforming him and bringing him into the conformity with Jesus Himself.

Little by little, Paul is saying, "Jesus is changing me so I look more and more like Him and less and less like my old self."

When I was a teenager, the phrase was, "You just think you're it, don't you?" This aptly described those who thought they were the hottest thing going. They were proud and self-sufficient.

That kind of self-sufficiency and self-reliance will get you nowhere. Paul is consumed with Jesus at work in his life, knowing that the resurrection power of Christ truly made it possible for him to be cleansed, to be forgiven, to be changed instantly into a child of God, and gradually more and more to look like Jesus, more and more to be able to bear the fruit of Jesus as our Lord.

> I press on toward the goal for the prize of the upward call of God in Christ Jesus.

Paul kept the goal in mind on a daily basis, but he was also aware of his ultimate destination.

Those who don't know their ultimate destination are going to have a hard time moving toward the goal. But when you know the destination, you are able to understand the application of pressing forward on a daily basis and letting Jesus be Lord of your life.

## Advice #5 — Help your fellow travelers along the way

Have you ever noticed that Jesus was never in a hurry? Yes, He was intentional, He knew where He was going, He had a clear picture of what life was about; but, He never seemed hurried. He always had time for the individuals He encountered along the way.

It is imperative that you and I learn this. We, too, must help our fellow travelers.

Now, I must admit that I'm a type A personality, and when I set my goals and determine where I want to go, I get so caught up in wanting to get there that I often lose sight of the opportunities of ministry along the way.

In my journey, I've seen this in my life and I've learned, and am still learning, not to blow past those moments. Instead, I should value them and embrace them.

> There are people who God puts in our path every day who He wants us to help.

We are never too important, never beyond recognizing that there are people in our path each day whom God puts there! He wants us to help them.

I really do believe the Lord is asking you and me to have a sensitivity to the people around us who need help, who need encouragement, and who need just a little bit of our time along the way.

Therein lies a huge part of the joy in the journey.

## Take action

- Now is always the time to take action.

- Get going, keep going, or get going, again.

- Don't camp too long in one place.

- Choose your companions carefully.

- Keep your destination and your goals clearly in mind.

- Help your fellow travelers along the way.

# CHAPTER 8

# Six Resolutions for a Joyous Life

Let's begin with a little quiz. On a scale of one to ten, where would you grade yourself as being a characteristically joyous person? I want you to think of ten as the absolutely joy-filled person, and one as a mean old codger.

Where are you on that continuum?

Pick a number right now.

Next, I want to ask you another question. Of those who know you best (i.e. your spouse, relatives, close friends, etc.), **how would they score you?**

Does that change things, or does the score remain the same?

> You want people to say that their life is better when you are close by.

I asked a church member how she was doing and she replied, "Better." I said, "That demands a little explanation."

She went on to explain that the person in her office who gave everybody grief was gone and she was better as a result of it.

How sad. Are people better off when you are around or when you are gone? I hope your mere presence is a blessing to others. That should be true for all of us.

## Six resolutions for a joyous life

When you know what to do but don't feel like doing it, the answer is to just do it. The feelings, the emotion, and the desire will follow your choice to do what is right.

Similarly, when it comes to living a joyous life, there are choices to be made based on the fact that they are right. You may not be in the habit, but that's okay.

Have you thought or said:

- I'm not sure I am characteristically a joyous person.

- It is a struggle for me to be joyous, and I know those around me would say the same thing.

- I would like to get better at living a joyous life.

- I believe, by God's grace, I can become a more joyous person.

I believe there are six resolutions we all need to memorize and to keep handy as we make the journey toward the life that God intends for us. It is this joyous life that will bless you and bless those around you.

## Resolution #1 — Resolve daily to live joyously

Joyous living is a daily affair, as Paul clearly stated:

> *Therefore, my beloved brethren whom I long to see, my joy and crown, in this way stand firm in the Lord, my beloved. Rejoice in the Lord always; again I will say, rejoice!* (Philippians 4:1, 4).

It is very important when you wake up in the morning for you to remember who you are and whose you are. Let these truths be the first thing you think about each morning.

> Remember who you are and whose you are.

Did you notice the language that Paul used in his letter? Twice he calls the people he is writing to his "beloved." He refers to them as brethren. They are family. They are the family of God, which means they share the experience of being brothers and sisters in a common cause in a common faith.

God also calls you His beloved. He loves you, and you need this truth to be burned deeply into your conscious and subconscious mind.

In addition, as part of His family, you can tap into the real joy of community, the real blessing of identifying yourself as part of the family of God. Not in a philosophical kind of way, but in a very tangible real way by being in a Bible study class, a discipleship class, a home fellowship with

> You will claim the joy that comes to you as a gift of His grace.

people whom you would have a name and a face, put together in a way in which you are connecting with them in a very real and wonderful way.

You know you are loved by them, that you are valued by them, and that you can call on them when you have needs. You can share the struggles and you can share the joys of your life with them. That's family!

Paul very subtly and briefly reminds us that we are the beloved of God and that we are family who shares the love of God.

He then goes on to say, and I paraphrase:

> **I challenge you on a daily basis to take your stand, to declare yourself as living this day in the very power of God's resurrected Christ.**
>
> **I challenge you not to allow the enemy, the nit-pickers, the economy, or the circumstances to overwhelm you or rob you of God's very best.**
>
> **You are to live as a child of the King, live in His victory, and claim the joy that comes to you as a gift of His grace.**

Joy is a gift that comes to us by virtue of the new life, the birth of Christ, by the Spirit of Christ living in us.

But it is also a decision.

God has given each of us a free will, and I believe it is imperative for you to say, "Lord, thank you for the ability to choose. And Lord, I choose today to claim the gift of joy. I will indeed rejoice."

Now listen. Paul makes it very specific. He said, "*Stand firm in the Lord*" and "*rejoice in the Lord.*"

You are not standing firm or rejoicing in what other people say to you today, not in the way your husband or wife treats you, not in the workplace, and not in what the economy is doing around you.

Rather, you are standing firm and rejoicing in the Lord, always. That is your daily resolution.

## Resolution #2 — Keep perspective

Many of you have read *The Purpose Driven Life* by Rick Warren. In it he tells a great story about a guide who worked at an art museum. His job was to take the people to the paintings, answer their questions, and then get out of the way. But the guide became increasingly obsessed with being the center of attention, even to the point that he would stand in front of the paintings so the only thing people could see was him.

> It is not all about you.

Clearly, the guide had lost perspective.

As Rick Warren so aptly points out, "It's not about you."

This simple truth is a required understanding in order to live a joyous life.

Paul wrote:

> *I urge Euodia and I urge Syntyche to live in harmony in the Lord. Indeed, true companion, I ask you also to help these women who have shared my struggle in the cause of the gospel, together with Clement also and the rest of my fellow workers, whose names are in the book of life (4:2-3).*

We don't know a lot about Euodia and Syntyche, but I suspect they are continually embarrassed in heaven when they have to explain exactly what the fuss was between them. Everybody's going to ask! Surely, if you can get tired in heaven, they would tire of the question. But we do know that their names are written in the Lamb's Book of Life. That's powerful, isn't it? Euodia and Syntyche were children of God, and they found themselves in a situation like many of us find ourselves.

Paul says that these two ladies "shared" with him in the struggle for the cause of the gospel of Christ. Now it is interesting to me that he used the past tense. At one time they had all shared a common cause, a common commitment, and they experienced the blessing and joy of being a part of something that was truly honorable and noble and bigger than themselves. And they weren't fussing and fighting during that time.

> Live for the honor and glory of Jesus Christ.

But somewhere along the way they got sideways with each other. Perhaps they stopped fishing and starting fighting. Or maybe they lost perspective and began to think it was about them. Perhaps they thought their opinion mattered the most, and that being justified in the eyes of their friends was more important. And then maybe the two women wanted others to line up alongside each of them and against the other.

Whatever the situation, it's clear that Euodia and Syntyche lost perspective.

If you want to live a characteristically joyous life, you will need to maintain perspective. Jesus said it was important for us to die daily to self. How's that for perspective?

It is not about us, but about living for the honor and glory of Jesus Christ.

Sadly, so many of us give up the harmony, give up the peace, give up the wonderful community that we experience with others over things that are trivial, unimportant, fleshly, and indeed, small.

Instead, we must choose to keep perspective by asking ourselves on a regular basis what is really important. Then, choosing to maintain our joy and our love for each other rather than letting little things bring division.

## Resolution #3 — Lighten up!

Though "Lighten up" is my translation, I do believe that is what Paul was saying when he wrote:

> *Let your gentle spirit be known to all men. The Lord is near* (4:5).

What is the normal temptation when you are under pressure, when people are squeezing you, when you feel as though you are under the gun?

Usually, we exert that same kind of pressure on those around us.

We must lighten up. We need to realize that:

- We don't have to be hard.
- We don't have to be difficult.
- We don't have to point out every shortcoming.
- We don't have to be so utterly demanding in life.

Let your gentle spirit be known. Does that mean you are no longer goal oriented? Does it mean that getting something accomplished is no longer important? No, it doesn't mean that for all you type A personalities; but, it does mean you keep in mind there is a right way, there is an effective way to move forward, to bring people along with you and not to alienate people in the process, to be able to reach a goal, and to have a higher sense of fulfillment in doing it.

> Let your gentle spirit be known to all men.

Paul said we should let our gentle spirit be known to all men, not just our bosses we are accountable to, not just the people we like, not just the people who like us, and not just our spouse when he or she is kind.

Rather, we are to let our gentle spirit be seen in all situations. Simply put, we must lighten up!

## Resolution #4 — Make prayer your first response

If you have not committed to memory Philippians 4:6, then you are in a fistfight with both hands tied behind your back. That means you are not very well prepared.

Paul wrote:

> *Be anxious for nothing, but in everything by prayer and supplication with thanksgiving let your requests be made known to God* (4:6).

I love the story about a village in Africa that came to Christ. The entire village was wonderfully transformed out of paganism and idolatry into a wonderfully vibrant walk with the Lord.

These men and women reportedly, because of their commitment to a devotional life and time alone with the Lord, had a separate place in the bush where they would

> It is absolutely contrary to God's will for you to be anxious.

pour out their hearts to the Lord. Over time, the paths to these places became well worn.

If one of these believers began to neglect his prayer life, it was soon apparent to the others. They would kindly remind the negligent one, "Brother, the grass grows on your path."

Well, it may not be so obvious from the wear on the carpet or the wear on the grass in our yard, but our neglect of prayer can't be hidden for very long. We think we are supposed to do everything in our power, exhaust all our resources first, to deal with the threats, to deal with the challenges of life.

Paul is saying that anxiety short-circuits the joy of life. Anxiety always causes you to take your eyes off the Lord, take your eyes off helping others, and causes you to become self-centered. Paul is saying it is absolutely contrary to God's will for you to be anxious.

Instead, every time there is a threat to your peace, every time there is something that short-circuits your joyous disposition of life, it ought to be the signal that says, "It's time to pray and to take it to the Lord."

In that context you can say, "Lord, thank you. I can look back in my life, and I can see the many other times I was threatened, the many other difficult moments in my life where You were faithful. And, when I would release myself and trust in You, You always made wonderful provisions for me."

Take it to God in prayer.

## Resolution #5 — Choose carefully what you dwell on

When it comes to living a joyous life, Paul's words make it very plain:

> *Finally, brethren, whatever is true, whatever is honorable, whatever is right, whatever is pure, whatever is lovely, whatever is of good repute, if there is any excellence and if there is anything worthy of praise, dwell on these things (4:8).*

Now what is the temptation? Well, it is for us to fret about what has happened in the stock market. If we are not careful, we will become glued to the television, we will continue to check the progress of the market, and our joy is directly tied to whether the fortunes or going up or the fortunes are going down.

Someone said their 401K is now a 201K. We understand that, don't we? All of us are affected by that. It is easy to become chronically anxious about financial things.

> **Fill your day with thoughts that are true, honorable, pure, and lovely.**

It could be problems in your marriage, problems with your in-laws, problems with your teenager, problems with your neighbors, the prospect of losing your job, afraid of getting old, or increasing debt.

Whatever it might be, if you are not careful, you end up dwelling on it, and you become compulsive in letting all of your energy go into those worries and those thoughts.

But Paul was saying that he had a better solution. He advised us to consider the things that are true and honorable and pure and lovely and to make it a point to fill our hearts and minds with these things.

Now that is good advice!

- When you become anxious, consider what is right.

- When you think the world is on your shoulders, think about what is good.

- When everything looks dark, think about what is true.

- When everyone around you seems to fall short of where they ought to be, think about what is pure.

- When you find yourself seeing the ugly, think about what is loving.

- When you awaken in the middle of the night gripped with fear, let your mind dwell on God's promises.

Paul's remedy is just as effective today as it was back then.


## Resolution #6 — Apply what you learned

This is the last resolution, but certainly not least. This is where the rubber hits the road, for if you tap into this, I guarantee you the other resolutions will have great lasting value.

> Action is required. Let that truth change your life.

When you apply what you learned, you see the change or growth that you want. Sadly, however, most people have the habit of filing things away. It's like they put the truth away in their mental attic … and never use it.

We must not do that. We must apply what we have learned and put it into practice. That is the secret.

In Henry Blackaby's *Experiencing God*, he explained that one of the ways we come to know God is by experience. As you obey Him and He accomplishes His work through you, the natural result is that you know God even more.

It's wonderful, but it requires action.

Look what it says: ... *practice these things, the God of peace will be with you* (4:9).

Not just at the church where you can visit Him on occasion, not just in the Bible where you can check in every once in awhile; but, when you are your busiest, practice the things you have heard and seen and learned.

When you practice them, the Lord is with you. He smiles at you. He is blessed to know that you are making the effort to incorporate these changes into your life. There is a sense of well being that comes over us when we know we are making the effort, when we know we are doing what we should be doing in the name of the Lord. Practice is the key to development; it is the key to progress.

> **Practice is the key to development; it is the key to progress.**

I tie my own flies for fly-fishing, but I tend to let months go by between when I pull out all the materials and all the little tools and begin to work on fly tying. A while back I decided I would tie some "Adam's parachutes." It shouldn't be that hard, but when you haven't practiced and you're working on something that is microscopic in size and you have great big old fingers like I do, it's hard. I looked at the first one I tied, and I was so disgusted. I thought, "If I were a fish I certainly wouldn't be tempted by that thing."

I wanted to just get up and walk away, but I stuck with it. I tied another one and it wasn't much better. I walked off and got a cup of coffee and came back and tied a couple more, and before long I was beginning to develop a little bit of the agility, a little bit of the nimbleness it takes to handle those small feathers and to do the things that were required on those tiny hooks.

Practice! Practice!

Or consider golf. I wish I could go out and shoot par golf. Someone said that Tiger Woods was once asked, "What is the most frustrating thing you hear?" His reply was very interesting. He said, "What's frustrating is when people say they would give anything to play like I play, but I know they are lying. They are not willing to put in the long hours that it takes to develop that kind of skill."

> Practice, practice, practice.

Again, it's practice.

If you want to live a life of joy, it is going to take practice, discipline, effort, and commitment. It means you are saying, "God, I've been taking in, I've been hearing, I've been listening. I think I've been learning. So, Lord, I ask you to help me know in a practical way on a daily basis what practicing these things looks like."

And for all of us, it means the moment we realize we've fallen short, that we confess it. It means we call on God's grace to cleanse us and let us start fresh in the process. And know that God is honored every time we do that.

## Resolve to keep your resolutions

These six resolutions need to be remembered. I suggest you:

- Put them over your mirror.

- Put them on your refrigerator.

- Put them on the dashboard of your car.

We all need to remind ourselves of the truth.

That is why we must do our part to remember the promises God made to us as to how we can live, how we can overcome, how He is faithful, and how He can provide.

Let your heart be filled with and anchored to the promises of God.

## Take action

- Now is always the time to take action.

- Resolve daily to live joyously.

- Keep perspective.

- Lighten up.

- Make prayer your first response.

- Choose carefully what you dwell on.

- Apply what you learned.

# CHAPTER 9

# The Joy of Soul Winning

The joy of soul winning is a joy that is available to each one of us, but Paul talks about this particular joy from a unique perspective.

He doesn't talk about the joy of evangelism or the joy of preaching. Instead, he talks about the joy of people.

Paul says:

> *Therefore, my beloved brethren whom I long to see, my joy and my crown ...* (Philippians 4:1).

Paul, in this short phrase, lets us in on a secret of joy he has experienced and that has made all the difference in his life.

## Looking a little deeper

I must mention that Paul makes almost the same statement in Thessalonians, and he spells it out there in a way that I think is going to help us make more sense of this passage.

He wrote:

> *But we, brethren, having been taken away from you for a short while — in person, not in spirit  — were all the more eager with great desire to see your face. For we wanted to come to you — I, Paul, more than once — and yet Satan hindered us.* **For who is our hope or joy or crown of exultation?** *Is it not even you, in the presence of our Lord Jesus at*

*His coming? **For you are our glory and joy*** (1 Thessalonians 2:17-20, emphasis mine).

And in Philippians, Paul wrote:

*Therefore, my beloved brethren whom I long to see, my joy and my crown ...* (4:1).

In both of these passages, Paul is saying he finds joy in people.

Yes, Paul has the joy of the Lord, he knows that joy is a gift of the Spirit that comes as a expression of the Holy Spirit being in control of his life, he understands that joy is evidence that Jesus is Lord and that he is walking with Him, he recognizes that he has to make a decision to be joyful and to tap into the source of joy ... but he is saying one more thing.

> When you've got Jesus, you've got the foundation for everything else, but you also need people.

He finds joy in people.

This may sound like a contradiction to a lot of what we hear. Haven't you heard people say, "All I need is Jesus?" After all, Jesus is the foundation for everything else.

But we do need each other; Jesus didn't call us to live in isolation. We need other people.

## Joy in people

But there's a little bit of a twist here that I think goes beyond the idea that we just need each other and that there's joy in our companionship and our fellowship. Paul was speaking to a group of people whom he had introduced to Christ.

A bond was made when these people became brothers and sisters in the family of God. Paul was the spiritual midwife, as it were, who helped them at the point of birth in their spiritual lives.

Because of that unique bond, Paul freely said:

- You are beloved.

- I long to see you.

- I look for every opportunity to be with you.

- I want to be a continual part of your spiritual lives.

- I want you to know I'm thrilled for you.

- I want you to know that I'm proud of you.

- I want you to know it is a joy for me to pour my life into you because I see what Christ is doing in your lives.

With those you lead to Christ, you will share the same joy.


## Wearing the right crown

Not only are the people he has led to Christ his joy, but Paul also calls them his "crown." He says it twice in both passages.

Consider the word "crown" for a minute. I don't see very many people wearing crowns these days. Maybe in a pageant at Christmas I might see someone with a crown, or my granddaughter wearing a tiara, but that's all pretend or for show.

What does Paul mean by "crown"?

There are two Greek words for crown, and it is very important for you to know which one he is using here. There's the Greek word "diadema" and that is the crown for royalty, like the crown a king wears. We get into real trouble spiritually when we try to wear the wrong crown. That crown is reserved only for Jesus, because He alone is Sovereign.

What keeps Jesus happy? Stay off His throne. Well, the auxiliary to that is, don't wear His crown. Don't make yourself out to be Lord. He alone is Lord. There is no room for you to try to share that crown.

> Make sure you're wearing the right crown.

When Paul calls these people his crown, he is in no way suggesting they take the place of the Lord or that they are a substitute for Jesus.

The other Greek word for crown is "stefanos." You see this type of crown at an athletic competition. The woven olive branches presented to the winner of a competition is a good example. It is a symbolic gesture, but one that is worn proudly.

Sometimes because of a great accomplishment, people are recognized. They bring value to a group of people and are presented with a crown. The crown is a way of saying, "You are significant."

Paul is saying the same thing. He is recognizing the value of his friend whom he is writing to and is saying, "You are my crown, my emblem of success. You have turned to Jesus. You have come to faith. You share with me a love for the Lord."

## Joy in what remains

Paul said:

> *For who is our hope or joy or crown of exultation? Is it not even you, in the presence of our Lord Jesus at His coming? For you are our glory and our joy* (1 Thessalonians 2:19-20).

Paul is saying something here that we need to hear carefully. **He is saying the things that most of us value in life are just going to fade away.**

In short, the things that most of us glory in have no lasting value. They will have no luster, no appeal to us, when Jesus comes again.

The one thing that will have the ultimate appeal, the one thing that we're going to value the most when Jesus comes, is the privilege we would have to put our arms around brothers and sisters and present them to Jesus.

> Everything on this earth will fade away ... but what is of God will remain forever.

Imagine the joy of being able to introduce them to the King of Kings and the Lord of Lords!

## The value and joy of finding what is lost

Jesus asked a very good question:

> *If a man has a hundred sheep and has lost one of them, does he not leave the ninety-nine in the open pasture and go out after the one which is lost, until he finds it? When he has found it, he lays it on his shoulders, rejoicing. And when he comes home, he calls together his friends and his neighbors, saying to them, "Rejoice with me, for I have found my sheep which was lost!"* (Luke 15:4-6).

Then Jesus removes all doubt as to the value and importance of lost people when He said:

> *I tell you that in the same way, there will be more joy in heaven over one sinner who repents than over ninety-nine righteous persons who need no repentance* (15:7).

The same idea is expressed in the next parable:

> *What woman, if she has ten silver coins and loses one coin, does not light a lamp and sweep the house and search carefully until she finds it? And when she has found it, she calls together her friends and neighbors, saying, "Rejoice with me, for I have found the coin which I had lost!" In the same way, I tell you, there is joy in the presence of the angels of God over one sinner who repents* (15:8-10).

God's love for the lost is unquestioned, and it is as if Paul is saying in Philippians and Thessalonians, "I have tapped into the source of joy that absolutely sets the angels in heaven on fire!"

That joy comes because Paul had the privilege of winning those people to faith in Christ.

And lastly, consider the parable of the prodigal son. When the son repents and goes home, acknowledges his sin, and asks for forgiveness, the father says:

> *"Quickly bring out the best robe and put it on him, and put a ring on his hand and sandals on his feet; and bring the fattened calf, kill it, and let us eat and celebrate; for this son of mine was dead, and has come to life again; he was lost, and has been found"* (15:22-24).

And what then did the people do? They began to celebrate!

That there is value in what is lost is not in question at all. **The question is whether we will experience the joy by finding what is lost.**

I believe there is a joy God has for us that we will not experience any other way, and once we have tasted it, once we really begin to experience that joy on a regular basis, we will never be the same!

It will change your life and your perspective. It will lift your spirit above the mundane and enable you to see who you are. That's pretty powerful joy!

## The joy of your master

Remember the story of the talents? The master entrusted three servants with a certain amount of money, or talents, and upon his return each servant reported how he had managed the talents.

To the servant who received five talents and multiplied it into ten and to the servant who received two talents and multiplied it into four, the master said the exact same thing:

> *"Well done, you good and faithful slave. You were faithful with a few things, I will put you in charge of many things; enter into the joy of your master"* (Matthew 25:21, 23).

What did he mean by "the joy of your master?"

I believe Jesus is offering us an amazing invitation to taste of the best of what God has to offer us. The joy of the master is seeing what he has given us multiply ... and what he has given us is Jesus.

> Never discount the power of God to speak through you.

The joy of the master is the joy of seeing others brought into God's Kingdom, and when we are instrumental in multiplying ourselves and bringing others into the Kingdom, we get to experience the same joy.

There are direct and indirect ways you participate in soul winning. You may pray for the lost or pray for the UPS driver on your front steps, you may give out a Bible or give a meal to your new neighbor, or you may support a missionary or go on short-term mission trips.

You may be thinking, "I'm not much of an evangelist." Please, never discount the power of God to speak through you to that person who is the clerk at store, to the one who does your yard, to the person who lives next door, or to a relative. Share what Christ means to you and talk with conviction in your heart. You know they need Jesus, even as you have needed Him. Trust in the power of God to do what only He can do to bring them into that saving relationship.

Whether you are directly or indirectly multiplying yourself, you are bringing joy to the master, and that is how you experience the joy of soul winning.

## Take action

- Now is always the time to take action.

- Find joy in people.

- Wear the right crown.

- Aim for the joy that remains.

- Find what is lost.

- Share the joy of your master.

CHAPTER 10

# The Joy of Contentment

Being content is truly a timeless message. The world, the media, and our very nature continues to demand more of everything — money, fame, pleasure, ego, image, you name it — yet Paul tells us we need the joy of being content.

Actor Brad Pitt once said, "I'm the guy who's got everything, I know. But I'm telling you, once you've got everything, then you're just left with yourself. I've said it before and I'll say it again, it doesn't help you to sleep any better and you don't wake up any better because of it."

There is no better time than the present to experience the joy of contentment.

## Content vs. Discontent

The concept of being content doesn't spark much passion. Maybe, in some ways, it almost seems to suggest a lack of ambition. It implies the idea that you are settling for what is rather than for what could be. It almost smacks of mediocrity.

> What comes to mind when you hear the word contentment?

Now consider being discontent. That has much more passion and emotion! I've heard it said that 80% of employees are dissatisfied with their current job. Divorce statistics tell us that marriage is rife with discontentment. And countless individuals have gone deep into debt to buy things they don't need and cannot afford, all in the pursuit of contentment.

The human race is far more discontent than it is content; but, that was never God's plan. And what's more, being content is not necessarily a sign of weakness, lack of ambition, or mediocrity.

## The benefits of contentment

Contentment is something we must value and want, because it will not happen by itself. You will need to go after it, work for it, embrace it, and claim it for it to become a characteristic description of your life.

> Every characteristic of contentment is also a benefit.

Interestingly, every characteristic of contentment is also a benefit we are able to enjoy, and that I am sure was God's intent. These four benefits can be yours if you want them.

## #1 — Contentment frees you from the disappointment of unmet expectations.

Without question for most of us, the single biggest issue of discontentment has to do with unmet expectations.

Many of us had, or still have, the expectation that:

- someone should have done something for us,

- someone should have valued us,

- we should have gotten a promotion,

- we should be married by now,

- our spouse should have been faithful to us but wasn't, or

- God should have answered my prayer by now.

On and on the list goes of all of the things that did not happen to us we think should have happened. It's just not fair! As a result, we are allowing ourselves to be robbed of our contentment and joy.

Paul made a point when he wrote:

> *But I rejoiced in the Lord greatly that now at last you have revived your concern for me; indeed, you were concerned before, but you lacked opportunity. Not that I speak from want, for I have learned to be content in whatever circumstances I am. I am amply supplied, having received from Epaphroditus what you have sent, a fragrant aroma, an acceptable sacrifice, well pleasing to God* (4:10-11, 18).

He was not suggesting that he was disappointed with the church at Philippi because they "at last" were concerned again for him. Rather, he said that he was honored and pleased that they revived their concern for him.

He was not fretting or complaining about being forgotten by the church in Philippi. Instead, he stated how thankful he was for their gift. He appreciated it immensely, but he was already content.

How does this affect us? What does this mean to you?

I believe the lesson here is that we need to be very careful that we are not empowering others to have control over the degree of contentment we are experiencing in life. Paul didn't blame the church in Philippi, he wasn't waiting around for their gift, and he wasn't upset that their gift finally arrived.

Paul was emotionally free because of his contentment. There is something very powerful, very beautiful, about being a person who lives with contentment and who is characteristically a contented individual.

> Be on guard lest others rob you of your joy.

Don't you like to be around people who are healthy, whole, confident, and kind? They are content, without question. They are not needy or hurting. Usually, in a good way, they rub off on you, encouraging you and building you up.

On the other hand, the damage and baggage that many people carry around is the result of discontentment. Their expectations were not met, and they simply can't seem to get over it.

Be on guard! Do not allow the expectations you may have of what someone else should be doing for you to rob you of your joy and your victory and your fulfillment in life.

Choose to be content.

### #2 — Contentment enables you to enjoy and value life for what it is, not for what you have.

There was a study by the University of Southern California that found that greater wealth did not translate into greater happiness for many of the 1,500 people surveyed over a 30-year period.

USC economist Richard Easterland said:

> Many people are under the illusion that the more money we make, the happier we'll be. But according to their study, that simply wasn't true. We know from other well-respected studies that fewer Americans are happier today than in the

1950's, despite having more money, bigger homes, and more stuff.

I believe contentment is a state of being at peace — at peace with yourself, at peace with God, at peace with the world around you. It means you have been able to set aside anger, to get out of the battle, the strife, and the rat race of life. It is the ability to enjoy life as it is.

Sadly, many of us are convinced that if we made more money, if we got a promotion, if we got married, if we got a divorce, if we had kids, if we didn't have kids, all of these things, or something else, would bring us what we do not have now.

But that is the myth! It's an illusion. The enemy wants to trick us into believing there is something outside of us, there is something yet to come that is going to produce in us what we have not yet experienced. Whatever that "something" is, it is always just out of reach.

> Contentment is the ability to enjoy life as it is.

Not so. Contentment is the ability to enjoy life as it is right now. It also includes appreciation for what you have.

Author Brennan Manning noted:

> I believe the real difference in the American churches is not between conservative and liberals, fundamentalist and charismatics, nor between republicans and democrats. The real difference is between the aware and the unaware. When somebody is aware of that love, the same love the Father has for Jesus, that person is just spontaneously grateful. Cries of thankfulness become thedominate characteristic of the interior life, and the byproduct of gratitude is joy. We're not joyful and then become grateful, we're grateful and that makes us joyful.

I think contentment is that state of being at peace, grateful, and joyful. It involves a sense of well-being and a sense of fulfillment. You are not lacking anything for you to experience God's best, God's blessing, and God's joy.

**#3 — Contentment gives you the strength to stand strong and not be swayed by the world.**

Listen to the words of the Apostle Paul:

> *I have learned the secret of being filled and going hungry, both of having abundance and suffering need. I can do all things through Him who strengthens me* (Philippians 4:12-13).

Contentment is the secret. Most of the world is clueless. The world doesn't understand how to be content. But Paul says twice that he has learned the secret of contentment.

It is interesting to me that a verse most of us who have grown up in the church or have been a part of the church for any length of time have come to treasure is Philippians 4:13: *"I can do all things through Christ who strengthens me."*

We love that promise, we hold on tenaciously to that thought; but, the context of that verse is found in the subject where Paul is learning how to experience contentment on a daily basis in his life, learning how to draw from his walk with God to be enriched and empowered and focused ... in spite of the circumstances around him.

> Most of the world doesn't understand how to be content.

Through Christ's strength, Paul was able to be content. That is the secret of contentment. We can't do it in our own strength. We need God's help.

The world is certainly not going to help you! Everywhere you turn, someone is trying to sell you something. You are bombarded with advertisements that try to tap into your existing discontent or try to create discontent so you will see the "need" for a new product.

Being content requires going against the flow, but don't let that stop you! Choose to be content, ask God for His help, and then take these practical steps:

**FIRST, keep your priorities straight.**

Matthew 6:33 says:

> *Seek ye first the kingdom of God, His righteousness, and all these other things will be added unto you.*

Not that I need to paraphrase the words of Jesus to help you understand them, but I think it is accurate to say when we seek the kingdom of God, when we seek the purpose of God, when we want to live by God's standards, we automatically place ourselves in a position where all these other things will fall into their rightful place. We will be able to see them for what they are. We'll be able to make good decisions about what we ought to pursue and what we shouldn't.

**SECOND, be spirit-filled.**

I'm not talking about speaking in tongues or some sort of ecstatic experience. I'm talking about what is the most basic, the most profound mark of the believer — the Spirit of the Living God dwelling in you as Lord of your life.

I would challenge you if you don't understand what it means

> When we seek the Kingdom of God, all things will fall into place.

to be Spirit-filled, to make it the single greatest quest for your life.

**THIRD, trust in God's plan, His provision, and His protection.**

Put your trust in Him because He is truly worthy of it. His Word is flawless and He cannot lie.

**FOURTH, do your best.**

Paul was not being arrogant when he looked at his life and said:

- I've fought a good fight.

- I realize I finished what God put in front of me to do.

- Deep inside I know there is a reward the Lord is going to give me, as well as a winner's crown because I have run the race to the conclusion.

Clearly, contentment is not mediocrity. It is not indifference. Contentment in its richest form comes to you at the end of the day when you lay your head on the pillow and you know you did your best. You gave of yourself fully to the purpose that God has called you.

## #4 — Contentment makes it possible for you to value what God is doing in the lives of others.

Paul wrote:

> *Nevertheless, you have done well to share with me in my affliction ... [But it's] not that I seek the gift, but I seek for the profit which increases to your account* (4:16-17).

In other words, contentment releases us from being caught up in ourselves, in our ambition, in our striving, and in what we want from others. Contentment allows us to have a perspective in which we value others and have a sensitivity to recognize the activity of God in their lives.

> **Contentment requires boldness, strength, and determination. It isn't for the weak.**

How do you relate to those around you? Do you try to keep things centered on yourself or are you able to be genuinely happy to hear that God is at work in their lives?

Not only is contentment a great benefit to you, but it is so rewarding to be around people who are content.

## Take action

- Now is always the time to take action.

- Get free from unmet expectations.

- Enjoy life for what it is, not for what you have.

- Stand strong against the world.

  - Have your priorities straight.
  - Be Spirit-filled.
  - God.
  - Do your best.

- Value what God is doing in others.

# The Goodness of God

The only way to know the kind of contentment God wants you to experience is to have a rock-solid, absolute assurance in your heart that God is good, that God loves you, and that God is on your side.

When you have that type of assurance in your heart, contentment is inevitable.

How do you get that assurance?

## #1 — Believe God's goodness is more than enough for you.

What does the goodness of God look like? Paul described the goodness of God extremely well when he wrote:

> *My God will supply all your needs according to His riches in glory in Christ Jesus* (Philippians 4:19).

If the goal of communism is to make everyone the same, then I assume it has accomplished that, but at the lowest level possible. Virtually everyone under communism finds himself living at a subsistence level.

For some people, that is their concept of the goodness of God. They believe, "Yeah, God will supply my needs, but it is going to be on a poverty level. He's going to dole out just enough beans and rice and sugar to get by."

The barest minimum is not God's plan! Paul said that God would supply all our needs according to His *"riches in glory."* God is not at the point of bankruptcy. God is not short in what He has available to us. He has more than enough for you!

## #2 — Believe that God rewards your faithfulness.

God rewards your faithfulness. A life well-lived for Him brings reward both in this life and in the future. Many of the parables of Jesus teach us about opportunity, accountability, and reward. God calls us, equips us, and blesses us when we obey and serve Him.

## #3 — Believe that God will use you for His glory.

God has great plans for you. He does, whether you are young or old, educated or uneducated, rich or poor, male or female, it doesn't matter because God is at work in you and through you.

Trust Him. Let Him be God.

## #4 — Believe that eternity will eclipse the good of today.

What awaits you in heaven for all eternity will completely over-shadow the things of this world. Think of the best moments in this life, the most satisfying events in this life, and understand they are God's gracious gifts, they are God's foretaste of what awaits you for all eternity.

## #5 — Believe that God is ultimately just and fair.

Many have experienced things in this life that were unjust and unfair, to say the least. But that reality cannot taint your view of God. He is just and fair.

The Apostle Paul understood the value and power of being content. In fact, I do not believe his life would have made the impact in the world that it did if he had not been content. Paul's witness and his words spoke of God's goodness, God's love, God's power, and God's strength in order for him to be content.

May you discover the joy of being content. That is exactly what you need for the journey of life.

# About the Author:

Pastor Mike Toby and his wife, Jackie, have been married for over forty years. Their two sons, Josh and Scott, are both married. Josh and Olya have two sons, Evan and Conrad; while Scott and Monica have one daughter, Marlena.

For the last thirty-two years, Mike has served as Senior Pastor of First Baptist Church of Woodway, a suburb of Waco, Texas. Under his leadership the church has grown to over four thousand members, has gone through eight building programs, including relocation to a new thirty-acre campus.

The church is widely known for its many ministries that touch all ages. It's passion for missions and taking Christ to the nations has impacted every area of the life of the church. Pastor Toby personally leads mission teams on a regular basis and is the cheerleader for others to be involved.

Pastor Toby's personal interests have long included a love for the outdoors, especially Colorado. Fly fishing and fly tying, as well as golf, have been more recent hobbies. Spending time with his young grandchildren is a special joy.

Mike can be reached at: mike_toby@fbcwoodway.org

# Paul J. Meyer's
# CHRISTIAN LIVING BOOKLET LIBRARY

Finding God's Will for Your Life

My Work Is My Ministry

Sharing Your Faith

The Journey of Prayer

The Joy and Responsibility
    of Stewardship

Fundraising – from the
    Donor's Perspective

Master Keys of Stewardship

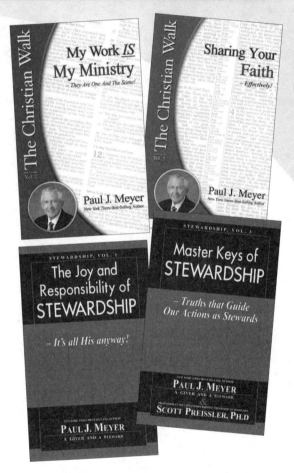

This special collection of 7 booklets by Paul J. Meyer will support and inspire
you through your daily Christian walk.

All booklets come shrink-wrapped in packs of 10. Keep some for yourself and
family members, and give away the others to those who you believe would find
inspiration in these uplifting booklets. Booklets are not available individually.

This Christian Living Booklet Library set is only: $42.

**To order visit: www.pauljmeyer.com**

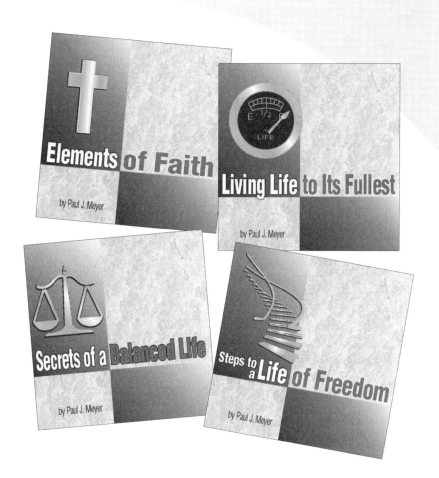

# Paul J. Meyer's
# TEEN DEVELOPMENT BOOKLET LIBRARY

That Something

Attitude Is Everything!

As a Man Thinketh

Personal Motivation

Self-Talk & Self-Affirmation

Successfully Managing the
   Time of Your Life

What Maims and Kills

Thank You, Mrs. McCormack

How to Find the Right Spouse

The True Role of a Leader

Being Smart with Your Money

This special collection of 11 booklets by Paul J. Meyer will help teens grow personally as they embark on life's journey.

All booklets come shrink-wrapped in packs of 10, which means you get 10 copies of each booklet. You can share or give away the other complete booklet libraries away as gifts! Booklets are not available individually.

This Teen Development Booklet Library set is only: $67.

## To order visit: www.pauljmeyer.com

# ORDER FORM:

_____ Library     copies X $_____ = $ _____

_____ Library     copies X $_____ = $ _____

_____ Library     copies X $_____ = $ _____

_____ Library     copies X $_____ = $ _____

Product Total $ _____

S/H $9/library set $ _____

Sales Tax (TX residents only) 8.25% $ _____

*E-mail customer service for international orders*

Name:_____ Title:_____

Organization:_____

Shipping Address:_____

City:_____ State:_____ ZIP:_____

Phone: _____ Fax:_____

E-Mail:_____

Charge Your Order:

[ ] MasterCard    [ ] VISA    [ ] AMERICAN EXPRESS    [ ] DISCOVER NETWORK

CC#:_____ Exp date:_____

[ ] Check Enclosed (Payable to PJM Resources)

**Paul J. Meyer Resources®**
PO Box 7411
Waco, TX 76714
Fax: 254-751-0475

**Email: ServiceTeam2@theleadingedgepublishing.com**